P9-ECV-382

Quest

Second Edition

Intro

Reading and Writing

Pamela Hartmann
Laurie Blass

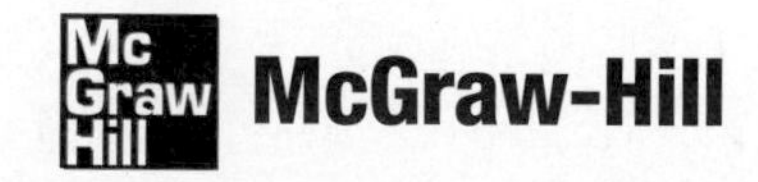

Quest Intro Reading and Writing, 2nd Edition

Published by McGraw-Hill ESL/ELT, a business unit of The McGraw-Hill Companies, Inc. 1221 Avenue of the Americas, New York, NY 10020. Copyright © 2007 by The McGraw-Hill Companies, Inc. All rights reserved. No part of this publication may be reproduced or distributed in any form or by any means, or stored in a database or retrieval system, without the prior written consent of The McGraw-Hill Companies, Inc., including, but not limited to, in any network or other electronic storage or transmission, or broadcast for distance learning.

2 3 4 5 6 7 8 9 VNH/VNH 11 10 09 08 07 06
ISBN 13: 978-0-07-312832-0
ISBN 10: 0-07-312832-5

1 2 3 4 5 6 7 8 9 VNH/VNH 11 10 09 08 07 06 05
ISE ISBN 13: 978-0-07-111923-8
ISE ISBN 10: 0-07-111923-X

Editorial director: Erik Gundersen
Series editor: Linda O'Roke
Production editor: MaryRose Malley
Cover designer: David Averbach, Anthology
Interior designer: Martini Graphic Services, Inc.
Artists: Jonathan Massie, Ron Mahoney
Photo researcher: David Averbach

International Edition ISBN: 0-07-111923-X
Copyright © 2007. Exclusive rights by The McGraw-Hill Companies, Inc. for manufacture and export.
This book cannot be re-exported from the country to which it is sold by McGraw-Hill. The International Edition is not available in North America.

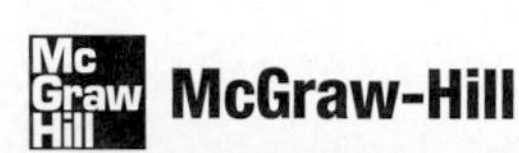
www.esl-elt.mcgraw-hill.com
The McGraw·Hill Companies

ACKNOWLEDGEMENTS

The publisher and authors would like to thank the following education professionals whose comments, reviews, and assistance were instrumental in the development of the Quest series.

- **Roberta Alexander,** San Diego Community College District
- **David Dahnke,** North Harris College (Houston, TX)
- **Mary Díaz,** Broward Community College (Davie, FL)
- **Judith García,** Miami-Dade College
- **Elizabeth Giles,** The School District of Hillsborough County, Florida
- **Patricia Heiser,** University of Washington, Seattle
- **Yoshiko Matsubayashi,** Kokusai Junior College, Tokyo
- **Ahmed Motala,** University of Sharjah, United Arab Emirates
- **Dee Parker and Andy Harris,** AUA, Bangkok
- **Alison Rice,** Hunter College, City University of New York
- **Alice Savage,** North Harris College (Houston, TX)
- **Katharine Sherak,** San Francisco State University
- **Leslie Eloise Somers,** Miami-Dade County Public Schools
- **Karen Stanley,** Central Piedmont Community College (Charlotte, NC)
- **Diane Urairat,** Mahidol Language Services, Bangkok
- **Pamela Vittorio,** The New School (New York, NY)
- **Anne Marie Walters,** California State University, Long Beach
- **Lynne Wilkins,** Mills College (Oakland, CA)
- **Sean Wray, Elizabeth Watson, and Mariko Yokota,** Waseda International University, Tokyo

Many, many thanks go to Marguerite Ann Snow, who provided the initial inspiration for the entire series. Heartfelt thanks also to Erik Gundersen and Linda O'Roke for their help in the development of the second edition. We'd also like to thank Dylan Bryan-Dolman, Susannah MacKay, Kristin Sherman, and Kristin Thalheimer, whose opinions were invaluable.

TABLE OF CONTENTS

TO THE TEACHER

Quest: The Series

Quest Second Edition prepares students for academic success. The series features two complementary strands—*Reading and Writing* and *Listening and Speaking*—each with four levels. The integrated Quest program provides robust scaffolding to support and accelerate each student's journey from exploring general interest topics to mastering academic content.

Quest parallels and accelerates the process native-speaking students go through when they prepare for success in a variety of academic subjects. By previewing typical college course material, *Quest* helps students get "up to speed" in terms of both academic content and language skills.

In addition, *Quest* prepares students for the daunting amount and type of reading, writing, listening, and speaking required for college success. The four *Reading and Writing* books combine high-interest material from newspapers and magazines with readings from academic textbooks. Reading passages increase in length and difficulty across the four levels. The *Listening and Speaking* books in the *Quest* series contain listening strategies and practice activities based on authentic audio and video recordings from "person on the street" interviews, radio programs, and college lectures. Similar to the *Reading and Writing* books, the four *Listening and Speaking* books increase in difficulty with each level.

Quest Second Edition Features

- New *Intro* level providing on-ramp to Books 1-3
- Redesigned, larger format with captivating photos
- Expanded focus on critical thinking and test-taking strategies
- Addition of research paper to *Reading and Writing* strand
- New unit-ending *Vocabulary Workshops* and end-of-book academic word lists
- Expanded video program (VHS and DVD) with new lecture and updated social language footage
- EZ Test® CD-ROM-based test generator for all *Reading and Writing* titles
- Teacher's Editions with activity-by-activity procedural notes, expansion activities, and tests
- Test-taking strategy boxes that highlight skills needed for success on the new TOEFL® iBT test

Quest Reading and Writing

Quest Reading and Writing includes three or four distinct units, each focusing on a different area of college study—sociology, biology, business, history, psychology, art history, anthropology, literature, or economics. Each unit contains two thematically-related chapters.

TOEFL is a registered trademark of Educational Testing Service (ETS). This publication is not endorsed or approved by ETS.

Chapter Structure

Each chapter of *Quest Intro Reading and Writing* contains five parts that blend reading and writing skills within the context of a particular academic area of study. Readings and activities build upon one another and increase in difficulty as students work through the five sections of each chapter.

Part 1: Introduction

- Before Reading – discussion activities on photos introduce the chapter topic
- Reading – a high-interest reading captures students' attention
- After Reading – activities check students' understanding and allow for further discussion

Part 2: General Interest Reading

- Before Reading – prediction and vocabulary activities prepare students for reading
- Reading – a high-interest reading at a slightly higher level than the reading in Part 1 allows students to explore the chapter topic in more depth
- After Reading – comprehension, discussion, and vocabulary activities check understanding

Part 3: Academic Reading

- Before Reading – prediction and vocabulary activities prepare students for reading
- Reading – a textbook selection prepares students for academic reading
- After Reading – strategies (such as skimming for main ideas, using a dictionary, and synthesizing) and activities give students the opportunity to use academic skills

Part 4: The Mechanics of Writing

- Chapter-specific writing, grammar, lexical, and punctuation boxes equip students to express their ideas.
- Content-driven grammar boxes are followed by contextualized practice activities that prepare students for independent writing assignments.

Part 5: Academic Writing

- A step-by-step model leads students through the writing process which may include brainstorming, narrowing the topic, writing topic sentences, planning the writing, and developing ideas into a paragraph.
- Writing assignments focus on a variety of rhetorical styles: chronological, description, analysis, persuasive, and process.
- Writing assignments ask students to use the writing mechanics taught.

Teacher's Editions

The *Quest Teacher's Editions* provide instructors with activity-by-activity teaching suggestions, cultural and background notes, Internet links to more information on the unit themes, expansion black-line master activities, chapter tests, and a complete answer key.

The *Quest Teacher's Editions* also provide test-taking boxes that highlight skills found in *Quest* that are needed for success on the new TOEFL® iBT test.

Video Program

For the *Quest Listening and Speaking* books, a newly expanded video program on DVD or VHS incorporates authentic classroom lectures with social language vignettes.

Lectures

The lecture portion of each video features college and university professors delivering high-interest mini-lectures on topics as diverse as animal communication, personal finance, and Greek art. The mini-lectures run from two minutes at the *Intro* level to six minutes by Book 3. As students listen to the lectures they complete structured outlines to model accurate note taking. Well-organized post-listening activities teach students how to use and refer to their notes in order to answer questions about the lecture and to review for a test.

Social Language

The social language portion of the videos gives students the chance to hear authentic conversations on topics relevant to the chapter topic and academic life. A series of scenes shot on or around an urban college campus features nine engaging students participating in a host of curricular and extracurricular activities. The social language portion of the video is designed to help English language students join study groups, interact with professors, and make friends.

Audio Program

Each reading selection on the audio CD or audiocassette program allows students to hear new vocabulary words, listen for intonation cues, and increase their reading speed. Each reading is recorded at an appropriate rate while remaining authentic.

Test Generator

For the *Quest Reading and Writing* books, an EZ Test® CD-ROM test generator allows teachers to create customized tests in a matter of minutes. EZ Test® is a flexible and easy-to-use desktop test generator. It allows teachers to create tests from unit-specific test banks or to write their own questions.

SCOPE AND SEQUENCE

Chapter	Reading Strategies	Writing and Writing Strategies
UNIT 1 EDUCATION		
Chapter 1 **Identity and Learning** • Introduction: *Stories of Twins* • General Interest: *You Are the Star of Your Own Movie* • Academic: *What Makes You the Person You Are?*	• Guessing the Meanings of New Words: Dashes • Finding the Main Idea • Understanding Parts of Speech • Guessing the Meanings of New Words: Definitions	• Focus: Paragraph Describing a Childhood Influence • Strategy: Choosing a Topic
Chapter 2 **Language and Learning** • Introduction: *Emailing a Professor* • General Interest: *The Brain, Learning, and Memory* • Academic: *Methods of Learning a New Language*	• Understanding Tone • Guessing the Meanings of New Words: Examples • Using Graphic Organizers • Guessing the Meanings of New Words: Parentheses	• Focus: Paragraph Describing a Good Way to Learn a Language • Strategy: Getting Ideas
UNIT 2 BUSINESS		
Chapter 3 **Deciding on a Career** • Introduction: *Career Questionnaire* • General Interest: *Where Am I, and Where Am I Going?* • Academic: *The Joy of Work?*	• Guessing the Meanings of New Words: Finding Meaning in Another Part of the Sentence or in Another Sentence • Understanding Pronoun References • Understanding Punctuation: Italics and Quotation Marks • Guessing the Meanings of New Words: Commas	• Focus: Paragraph Describing the Perfect Career • Strategy: Writing Complete Sentences

The Mechanics of Writing	Critical Thinking Strategies
UNIT 1 EDUCATION	
• Simple Present Tense • Simple Past Tense • Punctuation with *And* • Words in Phrases: Prepositions	• Applying Information • Comparing and Contrasting • Classifying • Estimating
• Using the Word *Or* • Punctuation with *But* • Words in Phrases: Words after Prepositions • Using *Because*	• Synthesizing • Recognizing Relationships Between Ideas • Applying Knowledge • Classifying
UNIT 2 BUSINESS	
• Future Tense • Possibility: *May* and *Might* • Using *Or* • Using *Enjoy* and *Involve* • Adverbial Conjunctions • Words in Phrases: Work	• Thinking of Solutions • Interpreting Information • Applying Information • Synthesizing

Chapter	Reading Strategies	Writing and Writing Strategies
UNIT 2 BUSINESS		
Chapter 4 **Marketing Across Time and Space** • Introduction: *Selling Movies* • General Interest: *Advertising Through History* • Academic: *Modern Advertising*	• Guessing the Meanings of New Words: Adjective Clauses with *Who* and *That* • Making Notes • Guessing the Meanings of New Words: Colons • Finding Examples • Recognizing Word Forms	• Focus: Paragraph Describing an Advertisement • Strategy: Writing a Paragraph
UNIT 3 SOCIOLOGY		
Chapter 5 **Parenting, Gender, and Stereotypes** • Introduction: *Parenting in Chimp Society* • General Interest: *Children, Gender, and Toys* • Academic: *Stereotypes and Their Effects*	• Guessing the Meanings of New Words: *In Other Words* • Infinitives of Purpose • Understanding the Word *So* • Previewing a Reading • Guessing the Meanings of New Words: The Phrase *That Is* • Finding the Main Idea: Using Topic Sentences	• Focus: Paragraph Describing an Important Lesson Learned as a Child • Strategy: Editing Your Paragraph
Chapter 6 **Becoming a Member of a Community** • Introduction: *Becoming an Adult* • General Interest: *Rites of Passage* • Academic: *Coming-of-Age Rituals*	• Guessing the Meanings of New Words: *Or* • Recognizing Key Words • Using Topic Sentences to Preview • Guessing the Meanings of New Words: Pictures and Captions • Finding Details • Understanding Words in Phrases: Verbs + Prepositions	• Focus: Paragraph Describing a Rite of Passage • Strategy: Rewriting Your Paragraph

The Mechanics of Writing	Critical Thinking Strategies
UNIT 2 BUSINESS	
• Present Continuous Tense • Simple Present Tense: Review • Subject-Verb Agreement • Showing Order • Adjectives • Adverbs • Words in Phrases: *It Is, There Is/Are*	• Applying Your Knowledge • Evaluating • Synthesizing
UNIT 3 SOCIOLOGY	
• Using *When* • Using *So* • Review of Conjunctions • Words in Phrases: *Used To* • Finding Words in Phrases	• Making Inferences • Understanding Cause and Effect • Comparing and Contrasting
• Review of Simple Present Tense • Review of Subject-Verb Agreement • Requirements: *Must* and *Have To* • Review of Showing Order • Prepositions of Place • Words in Phrases: Verb + Preposition Combinations	• Making Comparisons • Supporting Opinions with Experiences • Classifying • Synthesizing

Welcome

Quest Second Edition prepares students for academic success. The series features two complementary strands—*Reading and Writing* and *Listening and Speaking*—each with four levels. The integrated Quest program provides robust scaffolding to support and accelerate each student's journey from exploring general interest topics to mastering academic content.

New second edition features

- New *Intro* level providing on-ramp to Books 1-3
- Redesigned, larger format with captivating photos
- Expanded focus on critical thinking skills
- Addition of research paper to *Reading and Writing* strand
- New unit-ending *Vocabulary Workshops* and end-of-book Academic Word List (AWL)
- Expanded video program (VHS/DVD) with new lecture and updated social language footage
- EZ Test® CD-ROM test generator for all *Reading and Writing* titles
- Test-Taking strategy boxes that highlight skills needed for success on the new TOEFL® iBT
- Teacher's Editions with activity-by-activity procedural notes, expansion activities, and tests

Captivating photos and graphics capture students' attention while introducing each academic topic.

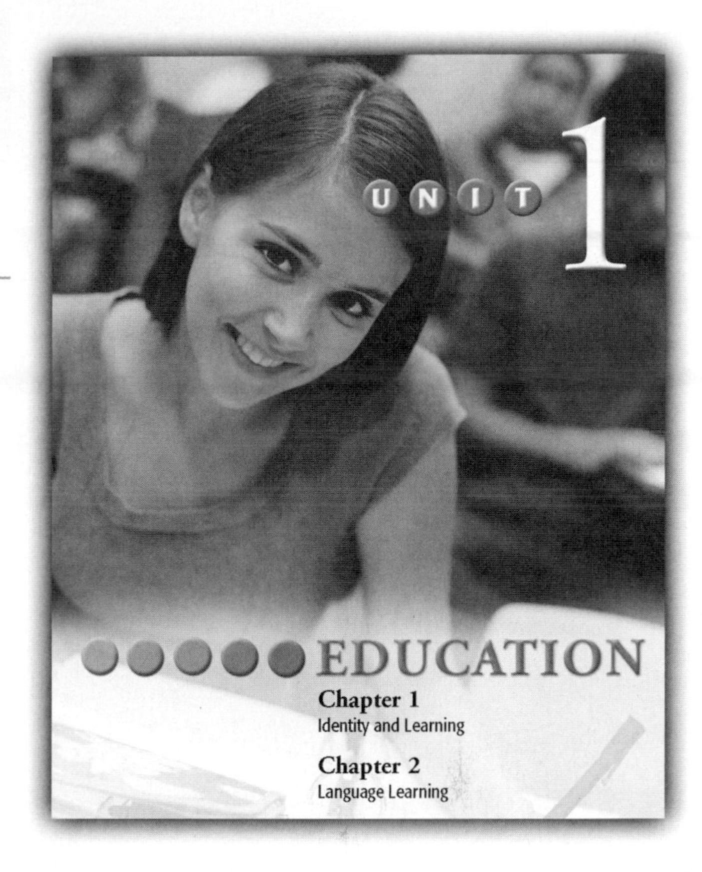

AFTER READING

A. CHECK YOUR UNDERSTANDING Which statements are true, according to the reading? Check (✓) the true statements.

1. Coming-of-Age Day in Japan celebrates the age when people have the rights of adults.
2. Coming-of-Age Day is becoming more popular.
3. The *quinceaños* celebration is a small, quiet, informal event.
4. In the *quinceaños* celebration, the tiara symbolizes the girl's childhood.
5. After *rumspringa*, most Amish young people leave the Amish community.

Reading Strategy

Finding Details

Details are specific information about a topic. They are usually facts, examples, or explanations. They usually follow main idea statements.

Examples: During *rumspringa*, Amish boys and girls can do whatever they want to do (**Main Idea Statement**). They drive cars, date, and watch TV. Many have big parties and stay up all night (**Details**).

B. PRACTICE: FINDING DETAILS Find details for these ideas in *Coming-of-Age Traditions*.

Ideas	Details
In Japan, 20-year-olds have the rights of adults.	They can vote and get married without parental consent.
For Coming-of-Age Day, young adults wear formal clothing.	
Fiesta de quinceaños is a very formal event.	
For the *quinceaños* celebration, the girl receives symbolic gifts.	
The Amish have strict rules.	
Most Amish teenagers return to the Amish way of life.	

154 UNIT 3 Sociology

Strategy-based approach develops reading, writing, critical thinking, and test-taking skills needed for academic success.

Three high-interest reading selections in each chapter introduce students to the course content most frequently required by universities.

READING

Read about movie titles. As you read, think about this question:
• Movies sometimes have different titles in different countries. Why?

Same Movie, Different Name

People around the world enjoy movies from other countries. Movies from England, the United States, France, and Japan are especially popular. However, to "sell" a movie in a foreign country, movie studios often get a local company (in the foreign country) to give the movie a new title. Sometimes the local company translates the title of the movie for the new country. Sometimes the company creates a completely new title. It is often a challenge to choose a title. Let's look at some examples.

Often the new title of the movie is identical to the original one. An example is the American film *Along Came Polly*. In Germany, the title was *...und dann kam Polly*, a direct translation. However, sometimes the movie makers do not translate original titles directly. Instead, they make changes that "sound" good in the foreign language. For example, the American movie *You've Got Mail* was *Yū gatto mēru* in Japan. The new spelling of the words shows how the English title sounds to Japanese ears.

Along Came Polly English and German posters

READING

Read about modern advertising. As you read, think about this question:
• How do advertisers reach consumers?

Modern Advertising

It's a fact of life: people who make products need to sell them. This was true in ancient times, and it's even truer today. The product might be beautiful, useful, or necessary. It might be useless junk. Either way, it must get from the maker to the consumer. Advertisers are always thinking of new ways to make this happen.

Advertising

Companies create products and services, give them prices, and then want to get them to consumers. To do this, advertising companies tell consumers about the price or special qualities (characteristics) of the products or services. Successful advertising influences people to buy something. It makes people feel that the product or service will improve their lives. One strategy of advertisers is to appeal to people's emotional needs: the need for love, the need to belong to a group, to feel safe, to feel good about themselves, or to feel better than others. For example, advertisers will suggest that a person who uses a certain shampoo will be popular. An ad for an SUV might target the need for safety in a dangerous world.

A sports utility vehicle (SUV)

Product Image

More importantly, advertising creates a product's image: the values that the consumer connects with it. The image might be youth, luxury, or energy. For example, advertisers might create an image of luxury for a certain type of car. They might show an upper-class couple driving to a luxury hotel in the car. The consumer thinks, "If I buy this expensive car, it means that I have a luxurious lifestyle." Consumers frequently buy a product for its image even more than for its price or quality.

Types of Advertising

Advertisers reach consumers in many ways: through TV, newspapers, direct mail, radio, magazines, the Internet, and outdoor advertising. They use different methods for different products. For example, they use TV commercials for common products such as food because TV commercials can tell a story. They

Gradual curve in each chapter from general interest to academic content supports students as they engage in increasingly more difficult material.

Discussion, pair-work, and group-work activities scaffold the learning process as students move from general interest to academic content.

PART 2 GENERAL INTEREST READING

Children, Gender, and Toys

BEFORE READING

A. THINKING AHEAD Read the questions below and think about them for a minute. Ask classmates for their opinions. Record their answers on the questionnaire (𝍸 = 5 people answered this, for example).

Questionnaire				
Who is better at these subjects in school?	**Boys**	**Girls**	**Both**	**Neither**
• math				
• language				
• physical education				
• reading				
Who usually enjoys these activities?	**Boys**	**Girls**	**Both**	**Neither**
• playing a game with a group of children				
• talking with a "best friend"				
Who enjoys playing with these toys?	**Boys**	**Girls**	**Both**	**Neither**
• a toy house				
• a toy airplane				

CHAPTER 5 Parenting, Gender, and Stereotypes 117

UNIT 2 VOCABULARY WORKSHOP

Review vocabulary items you learned in Chapters 3 and 4.

A. MATCHING Match the definitions with the words. Write the correct letters on the lines.

Words	Definitions
______ **1.** attract	**a.** a group of people who want to buy something
______ **2.** effective	**b.** show
______ **3.** ancient	**c.** It's too bad, but…
______ **4.** reflect	**d.** people who admire sports teams and players
__a__ **5.** market	**e.** look good to someone
______ **6.** unfortunately	**f.** get better
______ **7.** fans	**g.** male or female
______ **8.** improve	**h.** from very old times
______ **9.** income	**i.** successful
______ **10.** gender	**j.** money that people make from work

B. SENTENCE HALVES Match the first half of the sentences with the correct second half. Write the correct letters on the lines.

__d__ **1.** Name brand products are… **a.** attract consumers to their products.

______ **2.** We can acquire understanding… **b.** in chess.

______ **3.** By clicking a button,… **c.** ancient people.

______ **4.** Advertisers hope to… **d.** usually expensive.

______ **5.** She's an expert… **e.** from experts.

______ **6.** An archaeologist studies… **f.** you can buy almost anything on the Internet.

108 UNIT 2 Business

Unit-Ending *Vocabulary Workshops* reinforce key unit vocabulary that appears on the Academic Word List (AWL).

COMPREHENSIVE ANCILLARY PROGRAM

Expanded video program for the *Listening and Speaking* titles now includes mini-lectures to build comprehension and note-taking skills, and updated social language scenes to develop conversation skills.

Audio program selections are indicated with this icon 🎧 and include recordings of all lectures, conversations, pronunciation and intonation activities, and reading selections.

Teacher's Edition provides activity-by-activity teaching suggestions, expansion activities, tests, and special TOEFL® iBT preparation notes

EZ Test® CD-ROM test generator for the *Reading and Writing* titles allows teachers to create customized tests in a matter of minutes.

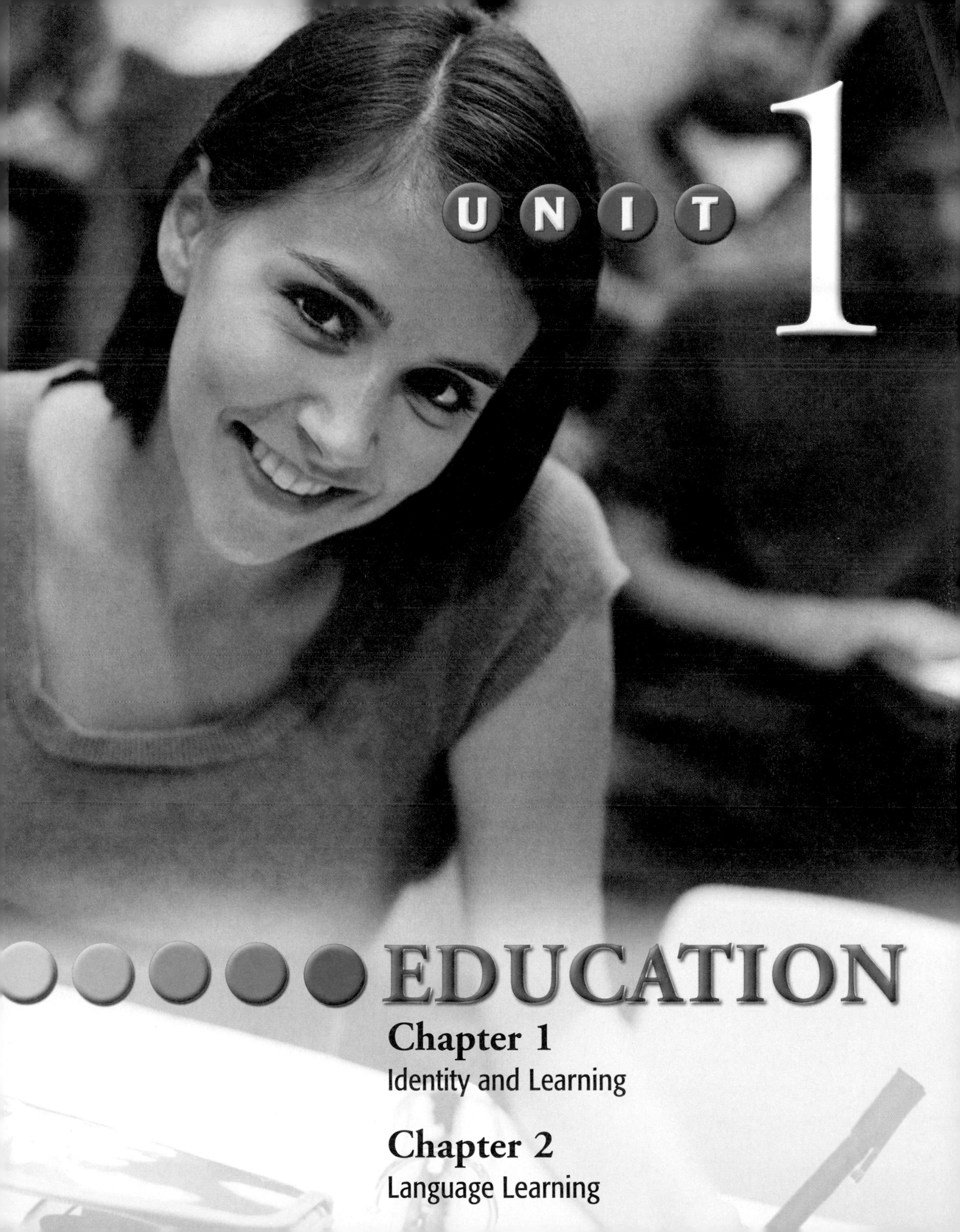

UNIT 1

EDUCATION

Chapter 1
Identity and Learning

Chapter 2
Language Learning

CHAPTER 1

Identity and Learning

Discuss these questions:

- Look at the picture. Where is the young woman?
- What do you study at school?
- Why do you study it? What are your future goals?
- Read the chapter title. What do you think the chapter will be about?

PART 1 INTRODUCTION Stories of Twins

BEFORE READING

Brothers and sister

Non-identical twin brothers

Identical twin sisters

THINKING AHEAD Look at the pictures. Then answer the questions with a partner.

1. Do you have brothers or sisters?
2. If you have a brother or sister, what are his/her favorite subjects in school? Foods? Movies?
3. Do you know any identical twins? Do you know any non-identical twins? Describe them.

READING

Read about two sets of twins. As you read, think about this question:
• What is surprising about each set of twins?

Stories of Twins

Mark and Gerald

Mark and Gerald are identical twin brothers. They met for the first time as adults. They didn't meet each other until the age of 32 because they were separated at birth. They looked identical—exactly the same. When they looked at each other, it was like looking in a mirror. But they grew up in different families. They went to different schools in different towns. They had different friends. So the brothers were very different from each other, right? Wrong! Each brother started to learn about the other. Both liked movies starring the actor John Wayne. Both liked the same sport—wrestling. And both had the same job—as firefighters!

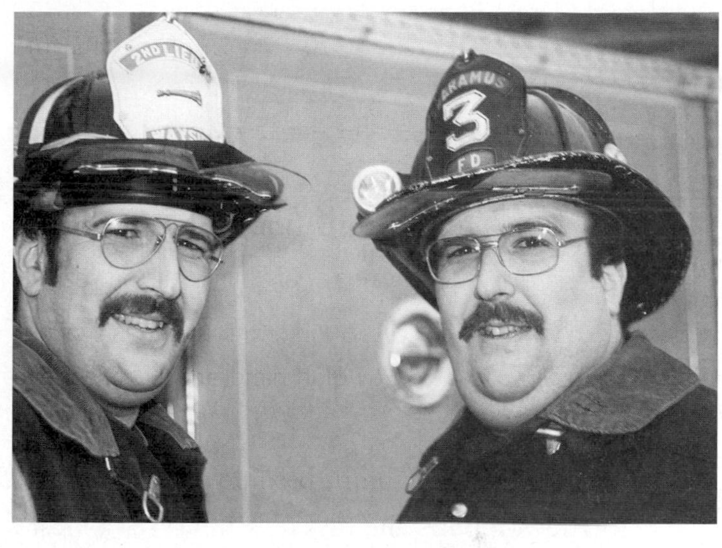

Identical twin firefighters

The Two Jims

Jim Springer and Jim Lewis are also identical twins. Like Mark and Gerald, they didn't grow up together. They grew up in different families and met for the first time 39 years after they were born. Of course, their appearance was the same: the same height, the same weight, the same hair color and eye color. But they noticed more. They also walked and moved the same way. Their likes and dislikes were the same. They drove the same kind of car. In school, they both liked math and disliked spelling. For vacations, they both enjoyed the exact same beach in Florida. And they both disliked baseball.

Twin Studies

Scientists can learn a lot from the study of twins. Our identity—our appearance and personality—seems to come mostly from our parents. Even twins separated from childhood are very much alike.

AFTER READING

A. CHECK YOUR UNDERSTANDING Which sentences are true? Which sentences are false? Fill in (T) for *True* or (F) for *False*.

1. Mark and Gerald look the same. (T) (F)
2. Mark and Gerald grew up in the same home. (T) (F)
3. Mark and Gerald have similar interests. (T) (F)
4. Mark and Gerald do the same kind of work. (T) (F)
5. As children, Jim Springer and Jim Lewis lived together. (T) (F)
6. Jim and Jim liked different things. (T) (F)
7. Appearance and personality are part of our identity. (T) (F)

B. TALK ABOUT IT Find a classmate with a brother or sister. Ask the questions below. Fill in the chart with his/her answers.

Examples: Is your appearance **the same as** your brother's (sister's)?

Are your likes and dislikes **similar to** (almost the same as) your brother's (sister's)?

Are your favorite classes **different from** (not the same as) your brother's (sister's)?

	The Same As	Similar To	Different From
Example: **Appearance:** (hair color, height, body)		✓	
Appearance (hair color, height, body)			
Likes and Dislikes (sports, hobbies, movies, books, music)			
Favorite Classes (math, English, science, history)			

PART 2 GENERAL INTEREST READING
You Are the Star of Your Own Movie

BEFORE READING

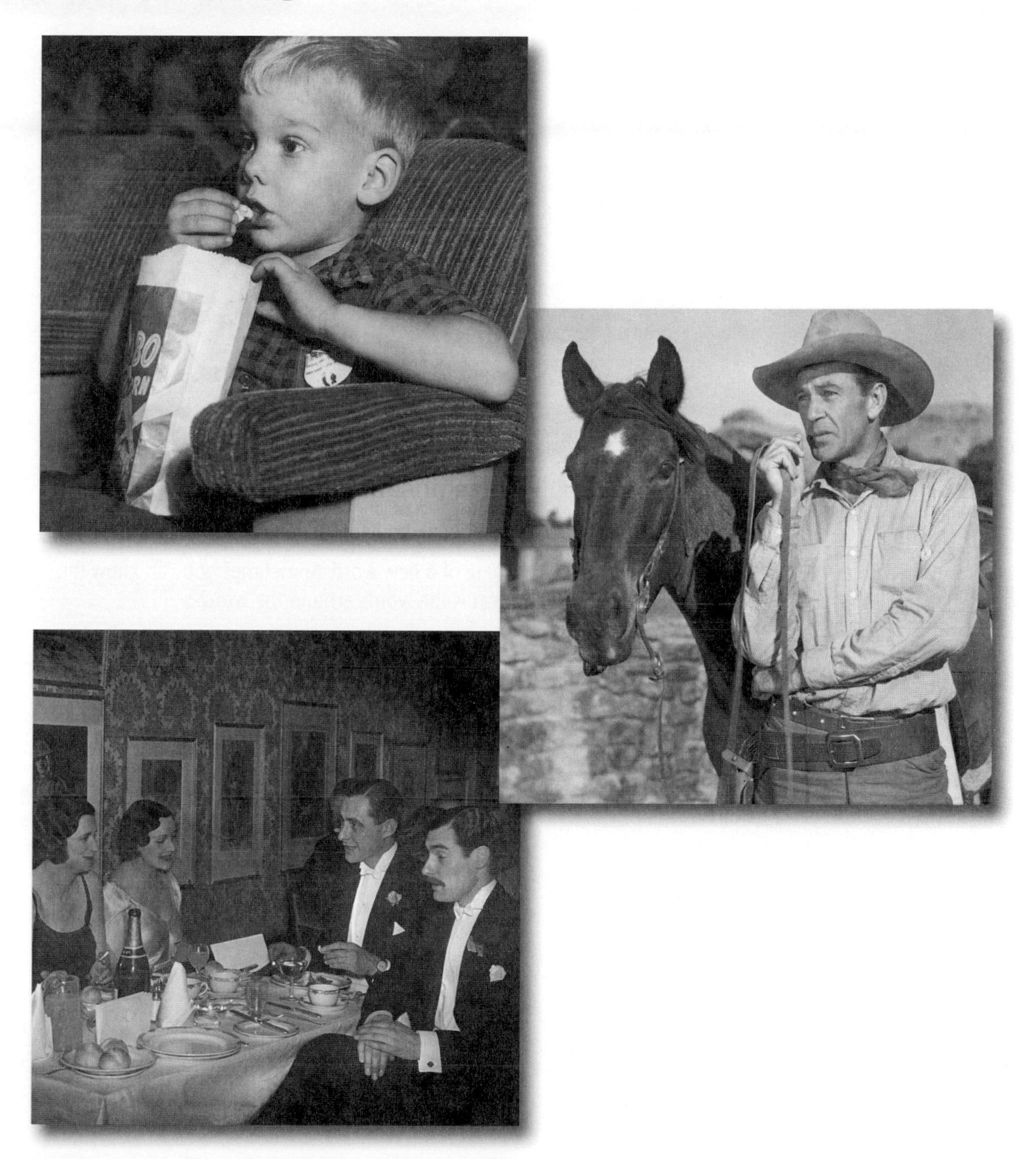

A. MAKING PREDICTIONS Look at the photos. What will the reading on page 9 be about? Discuss your answer with a partner.

B. VOCABULARY PREPARATION Read the sentences below. The words in blue are from the next reading. Match the definitions in the box with the words in blue. Write the correct letters on the lines.

a. anything	d. not poor	g. star
b. fun	~~e.~~ not strange	
c. not a child; a person over 18	f. plan and make	

___e___ **1.** Jim went to college. Then he worked in a department store. It was a **normal** life.

______ **2.** As a child, Ashley loved movies. As an **adult**, she still loved movies.

______ **3.** You can be **whatever** you want to be.

______ **4.** Blake started to **design** clothes. Now he has his own clothing business.

______ **5.** It's a movie about rich, **upper-class** people.

______ **6.** Josh is the **hero** of the movie.

______ **7.** Movies are a form of **entertainment**, like parties or TV or sports.

Reading Strategy

Guessing the Meanings of New Words: Dashes

You don't always need a dictionary to guess the meaning of a new word. Sometimes you can know the meaning of the new word from the **context**. The context is the words around the word.

Sometimes the meaning is after a dash (—).

Example: They looked **identical**—(exactly the same).

C. GUESSING THE MEANINGS OF NEW WORDS: DASHES As you read, notice the meanings of words after dashes.

READING

Read about designer Ralph Lauren and movies. As you read, think about this question:
- How is Ralph Lauren's life like a movie?

You Are the Star of Your Own Movie

Ralph Lauren, American fashion designer

Ralph Lifshitz was born in 1939. He grew up in the Bronx, New York, in a middle class family—not poor, but not rich. After high school, he studied business at City College in New York. Then he worked in a department store. It was a normal life.

But Ralph Lifshitz didn't want a normal life. As a child, he loved movies. As an adult, he still loved movies. He wanted to be like the actors. He learned something important in movie theaters: it's possible to "be whatever you want to be." At age 17, he changed his name to Ralph Lauren because *Lauren* is easier to pronounce and spell than Lifshitz. He began to design clothes: jeans and boots from cowboy movies and fine English suits from British movies about rich, upper-class people. He created his own company and became famous and successful. He became the hero of his own "movie"—his life.

Movies are big business. They are entertainment. But they are more than that. In his book *Life: the Movie,* Neal Gabler says movies change us in both small and big ways. Part of our identity—our idea of who we are—comes from movies. Movies teach us how to do things, how to *be.*

The actor Elizabeth Taylor describes actors as "shy"—a little nervous and afraid of people. But they learn to hide in their movie roles. They become different, not shy. In a similar way, Gabler says, all of us play roles in everyday life. We have many roles—as student, child, parent, friend, customer, worker.

It's an interesting idea. Your own life is a movie, and you are the star. You don't only play the hero of your movie. You create the whole movie. You choose the costumes—the clothes. You choose the scenes—places to live, go to school, or take a vacation. You choose the other actors—your friends, for example. Maybe most important is the plot—the story. You are also the writer of your movie, and you can choose to change the plot!

AFTER READING

Reading Strategy

Finding the Main Idea

The main idea is the "big" idea of a reading. It includes all other "small" ideas. Sometimes you can find the main idea at the beginning of a reading. Sometimes it is at the end.

A. MAIN IDEA What is the main idea of the reading? (Hint: In this reading, it is near the end.) Fill in the correct bubble.

- Ⓐ Ralph Lauren changed his life because of movies.
- Ⓑ Everyone has different roles in life.
- Ⓒ Your life is similar to a movie, and you can change it.

B. VOCABULARY CHECK Fill in the blanks with words from the box.

costumes	**middle-class**	**role**	**~~shy~~**
identity	**plot**	**setting**	

1. Jenny was ____shy____ and a little afraid of people.
2. Peter comes from a ____________ family in a small town. His family is not rich or poor.
3. John Wayne often played the ____________ of a cowboy in old movies.
4. Movies give us ideas about who we are. Neal Gabler thinks part of our ____________ comes from movies.
5. The ____________ in the movie were very beautiful long dresses and fine suits.
6. In the ____________ of the movie, a young man goes to Miami and tries to become a firefighter.
7. The ____________ of the movie is Hawaii.

Reading Strategy

Understanding Parts of Speech

Good readers need to understand **parts of speech**. When you know the part of speech of a new word, it's easier to guess meaning from context. Some parts of speech are **nouns, verbs,** and **adjectives**.

Parts of Speech	Examples
A **noun** (n.) is a person, place, or thing.	school height mirror firefighter
An **adjective** (adj.) describes a noun.	different favorite similar identical
A **verb** (v.) shows action.	am/is/are walks notice separated

Examples: The boys (n.) lived (v.) in different (adj.) towns (n.).

The brothers (n.) enjoy (v.) the same (adj.) beach (n.).

C. WORKING WITH WORDS Look at Exercise B on page 10. Decide the part of speech (noun, adjective, or verb) for each word you wrote on the lines.

Critical Thinking Strategy

Applying Information

Students often need to **apply** information. For example, they read about a situation, and they think, "What does this information mean to me? What is the connection between this situation and me?"

D. APPLICATION Read about Ana's life. Then describe *your* life as a movie. Fill in the box on page 13 with information about your life.

My Life, the Movie

Star: Ana Sanchez

Scenes: a small town in Mexico, New York City, a classroom at City College, a restaurant in New York

Costumes: mostly jeans and T-shirts, sometimes dresses

Actors: parents, brother, grandmother, friends in Mexico (Susana, Lidia, Pablo), friends in New York (Alex, Kimi)

Music: salsa, rap, classic rock

Plot: A young woman from a middle-class family moves from her small town in Mexico to New York City. She is alone and a little afraid. She begins taking classes. She makes two new friends. She also gets a job at a restaurant.

Possible Plot Changes:

1. She goes back to Mexico and goes to college.
2. She stays in New York and studies fashion design.
3. She moves to San Francisco and falls in love with an actor.

My Life, the Movie

Star: ______________________________

Scenes: ______________________________

____

Costumes: ______________________________

Actors: ______________________________

____

Music: ______________________________

Plot: ______________________________

____

____

____

____

____

____

____

____

Possible Plot Changes:

1. ______________________________
2. ______________________________
3. ______________________________

E. DISCUSSION Talk about what you wrote in small groups.

PART 3 ACADEMIC READING

What Makes You the Person You Are?

BEFORE READING

A. MAKING PREDICTIONS Part of the next reading is about how family influences personality. For example, some people say the oldest child in a family is more independent and the youngest child is more dependent. What do you think the reading will say? Complete the sentences below with words from the box. Then compare your sentences with a partner's sentences.

CHARACTERISTICS

careful	**friendly**	**a hard worker**	**outgoing (likes to be with people)**
creative (likes to make things)	**happy**	**a leader**	**serious**

1. The first (oldest) child in a family is usually ______________ and ______________.

2. The middle child in a family is usually ______________ and ______________.

3. The last (youngest) child in a family is usually ______________ and ______________.

B. THINKING AHEAD Think about your personality characteristics. In your opinion, where did these characteristics come from? How much of you came at birth, from your parents? How much comes from life experiences? Write notes to explain your answers in the chart. Then share your answers with a partner.

Your characteristics	Percentage at birth, from parents	Percentage from life experience family, friends, education, etc.
Example: Appearance	80%—my looks, how tall I am	20%—my haircut, my clothes
Appearance		
Likes/Dislikes		
Favorite Subjects in School		
Choice of Profession/Job		
Personality		

C. VOCABULARY PREPARATION Read the sentences below. The words in blue are from the next reading. Match the definitions on the right with the words in blue. Write the correct letters on the lines.

b 1. We **inherit** genes from our parents. We have them before we are born. — a. decide

___ 2. Genes **determine** hair color, eye color, height, and much more. — ~~b.~~ receive

___ 3. Non-identical twins **share** only 50 percent of their genes. Identical twins have all of the same genes. — c. have the same

Reading Strategy

Guessing the Meanings of New Words: Definitions

You don't always need a dictionary to guess the meaning of a new word. Sometimes there is a complete definition of the word within the reading. Look for definitions after *is, are,* or *means*.

Example: What is more important, nature or nurture? **Nature is** (biology, genes, or DNA.)

D. PRACTICE: GUESSING THE MEANINGS OF NEW WORDS: DEFINITIONS As you read, look for a definition of *nurture*.

READING

Read about identity. As you read, think about this question:
• Which is more important, nature or nurture?

What Makes You the Person You Are?

You have your mother's eyes and your father's ears. Your sister has your mother's hair color and your father's nose. You both have your father's mouth.

5 We all inherit these characteristics from our parents. But what about personality? What if one child is shy and another is energetic? What if one is good at music and the other is good at sports? Where do 10 these characteristics come from?

Genes in a DNA molecule

Nature or Nurture?

It's an old question: What makes us the people we are? Which is more important, nature or nurture? Nature is genes or DNA—biology. We receive these genes from our parents at birth. Genes determine hair 15 color, eye color, height, and much more. *Nurture* means life experience and environment. Education, family, friends, books, movies, and culture are all part of nurture.

Twin Studies and Nature

Scientists study both identical and non-identical twins. Identical twins have the same genes. Non-identical twins share only 50 percent of their genes. 20 When twins grow up together (as they usually do) in the same home, their environment is similar. But sometimes they are separated. They grow up in different homes and have different environments (nurture).

Genes determine characteristics such as eye color. We already know this. But scientists now know that genes—nature—also influence personality. Identity is not 25 simple. There isn't just one gene for every personality characteristic. For example, there isn't one gene for shyness, one for intelligence, one for happiness. Many genes together form a characteristic like being happy.

How Many Genes?

Each person has only 30,000 genes. That doesn't seem like many! But think of this: The alphabet has only 26 letters (A–Z). These 26 letters can form 30 a simple sentence ("Remember to call John") or a work by Shakespeare, the famous English writer. The number of genes isn't important. However, the combination of genes—how they are put together—is important.

What About Nurture?

There is good news: genes don't determine everything. Your environment is important, too. The people around you, school, experiences, and even birth order are all part of this environment. For example, you may have "musical genes," but you probably cannot play the piano without lessons.

Birth Order

Are you the first child in your family? Second? Third? Are you the only child (no brothers or sisters)? This birth order is part of your environment. A new study from Stanford University in California shows us something interesting. Birth order has an influence on personality. The oldest (first) child is usually a careful, hard worker and often a leader. The middle child is usually friendly and loves to be with other people. The youngest (last) child likes to create new things. A child without brothers or sisters often likes to be with adults, not just children.

Nature and Nurture

Nature determines about 50 percent of the person you are. Nurture determines the other 50 percent. One scientist talks about the "dance" between nature and nurture. Everything begins with nature. But experience and education—nurture—"turn on" genes (like a radio!). Then genes lead you to look for certain experiences. Together, both nature and nurture make you the person you are.

AFTER READING

A. MAIN IDEA The main idea of this reading was in one sentence.

1. Is that sentence at the beginning or the end? ______________________________

2. Write the sentence that gives the main idea. ______________________________

____

B. FINDING DETAILS Which sentences are true? Which sentences are false? Fill in (T) for *True* or (F) for *False*.

1. Characteristics such as eye color, ears, and hair color come 50 percent from nature and 50 percent from nurture. (T) (F)
2. *Nurture* means life experience and environment. (T) (F)
3. Nature does not influence personality. (T) (F)
4. Many genes together probably form a characteristic. (T) (F)
5. Birth order influences personality. (T) (F)

C. DISCUSSION Find classmates with the same family position as you—first child, middle child, last child, or only child. Discuss these questions in small groups.

1. What are some characteristics of your personality?
2. Do you share these characteristics with your group members?
3. Do you like your position (oldest, middle, youngest) in your family? Why or why not?

D. JOURNAL WRITING Choose *one* of these topics:

- twins
- changing your life
- your position in the family
- one of your personal characteristics
- an important influence on your life

Write about this topic for five minutes. Don't worry about grammar. Don't use a dictionary.

PART 4 THE MECHANICS OF WRITING

In Part 5, you will write about one influence on your life. You will need to use the present and past tenses, the word *and*, and some prepositions. Part 4 will help you learn how to use these.

Simple Present Tense

Use the simple present tense for the following:

1. general or permanent situations
2. repeated actions

Examples: Identical twins **share** 100 percent of their genes.

He **goes** to the same beach every summer.

Add an *–s* for the third person singular tense (for example, *Jim, he, she, it*). Spelling rules for words with *–s* are on page 168.

Two common irregular verbs are **be** and **have**.

BE:	I **am**	We **are**
	You **are**	They **are**
	He/She/It **is**	
HAVE:	I **have**	We **have**
	You **have**	They **have**
	He/She/It **has**	

For the negative, add the verb *do* + *not* to the simple form of the verb.

Examples: Non-identical twins **do not share** 100 percent of their genes.

She **does not have** a brother.

Contractions are common: **don't share, doesn't have**

A. SPELLING Use the spelling rules on page 168. Write the third person singular (-*s*) form of each verb.

1. like likes
2. enjoy ______
3. teach ______
4. learn ______
5. play ______
6. share ______
7. grow ______
8. do ______
9. dance ______
10. watch ______

B. PRACTICE: THE SIMPLE PRESENT TENSE Fill in the blanks with the correct forms of the verbs in parentheses.

Kim and Stacy ___are___ (1) (be) non-identical twin sisters. They __________ (2) (look) similar, but they __________ (3) (have) very different interests. Kim __________ (4) (like) sports. She __________ (5) (run) almost every day. On weekends, she __________ (6) (play) tennis or __________ (7) (go) swimming. Stacy __________ (8) (not like) sports. She __________ (9) (stay) up late and __________ (10) (watch) old movies on TV. On weekends, she __________ (11) (teach) dancing to children. The sisters also have different personalities. Kim __________ (12) (be) outgoing and energetic. Stacy __________ (13) (be) careful and a little shy. But they __________ (14) (share) one characteristic: they both __________ (15) (love) to travel.

The Simple Past Tense

Use the simple past tense for an action that started and ended before now. There are two forms of verbs in the simple past tense:

- Most verbs are regular. Just add *–ed* to the simple form of the verb.

Examples: He **worked** in a department store.
Movies **changed** his life.

- Many verbs are irregular. (See page 170 for a list of irregular verbs.)

Examples: They **met** at age 32.
He **became** a fashion designer.

Note: Spelling rules for past tense verbs are on page 168.

For the negative, add the verb *did* + *not* to the simple form of the verb.

Example: She **did not have** a brother.

The contraction *didn't* is common.
Example: She **didn't** have a brother.

C. PRACTICE: THE SIMPLE PAST TENSE Fill in the blanks with the correct forms of the verbs in parentheses.

My big brother ___was___ (1) (be) an important influence on me as a small child. I ____________ (2) (follow) him everywhere. I ____________ (3) (do) whatever he ____________ (4) (do). He ____________ (5) (join) the high school baseball team, so I ____________ (6) (play) baseball with the kids at my school. One year, he ____________ (7) (wear) cowboy boots, so I ____________ (8) (want) the same boots. He ____________ (9) (read) books, so I ____________ (10) (try) to read the same books. I probably ____________ (11) (bother) him a lot, but he ____________ (12) (not get) angry with me. When he ____________ (13) (go) away to college, he ____________ (14) (give) me his baseball glove. He ____________ (15) (be) my hero.

Punctuation with the Word *And*

With the word *and*, sometimes there is a comma, and sometimes there isn't. Use a comma to connect two complete sentences and when there is a series of items (a, b, and c). Notice the punctuation in these sentences.

Examples:

He became rich **and** successful.	no comma
Mark **and** Gerald are twins.	no comma
They walked **and** moved in the same way.	no comma
She's a wife, mother, **and** friend.	comma before *and*
Ralph changed his name, **and** he began to design clothes.	comma before *and*
He changed his name **and** began to design clothes.	no comma

D. PRACTICE: PUNCTUATION WITH THE WORD *AND* On a separate piece of paper, combine these sentences. Use the word *and* in each combination.

1. I like baseball. I like wrestling. I like baseball and wrestling.
2. Nature is important. Nurture is important.
3. Ralph designed jeans. He designed boots. He designed suits.
4. Education is part of nurture. Family is part of nurture. Culture is part of nurture.
5. My brother played tennis. My sister played soccer.
6. I went to the movie. I liked it a lot.
7. Mary and Kim are the same height. They are the same weight. They have the same hair color.
8. Mike and John grew up in different towns. They went to different schools.
9. Jessie is shy. She is musical. She is intelligent.
10. One sister is a teacher. The other sister is a designer.

Words in Phrases: Prepositions

As you read, notice words in phrases—small groups of words. For example, a phrase sometimes includes a preposition after a noun, verb, adjective, or other word. Some examples of prepositions are *of, on, about, to, in, for,* and *from*.

Examples: They **went to** different schools.

They like the same **kind of** movies.

Begin to learn these phrases. In this way, reading will help your grammar and vocabulary.

E. PRACTICE: FINDING WORDS IN PHRASES Read these sentences. Circle each preposition and underline the word before it. Then write the part of speech (noun, adjective, or verb) above the underlined word.

1. My grandmother was an important influence (noun) on me.
2. Jill is interested in costume design.
3. I'm very different from my sister.
4. Kirk's not very similar to his brother.
5. Harrison Ford is the hero of that action movie.
6. Movies are a form of entertainment.
7. A combination of nature and nurture makes us the people we are.

8. The small child was a little afraid of people.

9. Laura told stories about her trips.

10. Ben and Shelly talked about the importance of both nature and nurture.

F. REVIEW: EDITING A PARAGRAPH There are seven mistakes in this paragraph. They are mistakes with tense, punctuation, and prepositions. Find and correct them.

The actress Audrey Hepburn was an influence of me as a child. I loved her old movies. She seemed very different ~~of~~ from people in my life. She was beautiful, and elegant. She have a wonderful accent. After I see her in one movie, I wanted my hair and clothes to be similar hers. She was a lovely lady and I wanted to be like her.

PART 5 ACADEMIC WRITING

WRITING ASSIGNMENT

In Part 5, you will write one paragraph to answer this question:
• Who was an important influence on you as a child?

MODEL

Here is a model of one student's work. First, just read the model. Don't write anything yet. You will follow these same steps beginning on page 26.

STEP A. CHOOSING A TOPIC Who was an important influence on you as a child? Check (✓) one. Write who the person is.

- ☐ my parents—mother, father, or both ______
- ☐ a brother or sister ______
- ☑ another relative my grandmother
- ☐ a friend ______
- ☐ a famous person ______

STEP B. GETTING IDEAS Answer these questions. Write only short notes.

1. What was one characteristic of this person? interested in the world
2. What are three examples of this characteristic? traveled to Egypt, Hawaii, and Alaska
3. How did this person influence you? listened to her stories
4. What is this person's influence on you today? travel

STEP C. WRITING COMPLETE SENTENCES Use your answers from Steps A and B. Write them in complete sentences. Don't worry about spelling and grammar mistakes. (**Note:** There are some mistakes in the model sentences below.)

• Who was an important influence on you as a child?

My grandmother was an important influence to me as a child.

• Write your notes from Step B as complete sentences.

1. She was interesting on everything and wanted to learn about the world.
She love to travel, and the stories about her trips was wonderful.

2. a. For example, she go to Egypt, and rode a camel around the pyramids.

b. In Hawaii, she swam and surfed.

c. In Alaska, she climb mountains.

3. I listened to her stories and wanted to travel, too.

4. Today, I love to travel because of her influence.

STEP D. WRITING YOUR PARAGRAPH On a separate piece of paper, copy your sentences from Step C. Use paragraph form. Indent the first line. After each period, continue on the same line. Don't worry about mistakes.

My grandmother was an important (influence to) me as a child. She was interesting on everything and wanted to learn about the world. She (love) to travel and the stories about her trips (was) wonderful. For example, she (go) to Egypt(, and) rode a camel around the pyramids. In Hawaii, she swam and surfed. In Alaska, she (climb) mountains. I listened to her stories and wanted to travel, too. Today, I love to travel because of her influence.

STEP E. EDITING Read your paragraph and look for mistakes with:

- prepositions
- tenses
- the use of *and*

STEP F. REWRITING Write your paragraph again, without the mistakes.

My grandmother was an important influence on me as a child. She was interested in everything and wanted to learn about the world. She loved to travel, and the stories about her trips were wonderful. For example, she went to Egypt and rode a camel around the pyramids. In Hawaii, she swam and surfed. In Alaska, she climbed mountains. I listened to her stories and wanted to travel, too. Today, I love to travel because of her influence.

YOUR TURN

Now follow Steps A-F to write your own paragraph about this question:
• Who was an important influence on you as a child?

Writing Strategy

Choosing a Topic

Often, you will have a choice of topic. It's important to choose carefully. Choose your topic based on two factors:

• you know it well;

• you have information about it.

STEP A. CHOOSING A TOPIC Who was an important influence on you as a child? Check (✓) one. Write who the person is.

- ☐ my parents—mother, father, or both ______________________________
- ☐ a brother or sister ______________________________
- ☐ another relative ______________________________
- ☐ a friend ______________________________
- ☐ a famous person ______________________________

STEP B. GETTING IDEAS Answer these questions. Write only short notes.

1. What was one characteristic of this person? ______________________________
2. What are three examples of this characteristic? ______________________________
3. How did this person influence you? ______________________________
4. What is this person's influence on you today? ______________________________

STEP C. WRITING COMPLETE SENTENCES Use your answers from Steps A and B. Write them in complete sentences. Don't worry about spelling and grammar mistakes.

- Who was an important influence on you as a child? ______________________________

- Write your notes from Step B as complete sentences.

1. ______________________________

2. a. ______________________________

   b. ______________________________

   c. ______________________________

3. ______________________________

4. ______________________________

STEP D. WRITING YOUR PARAGRAPH On a separate piece of paper, copy your sentences from Step C. Use paragraph form. Indent the first line. After each period, continue on the same line. Don't worry about mistakes.

STEP E. EDITING Read your paragraph and look for mistakes with:

- prepositions
- tenses
- the use of *and*

STEP F. REWRITING Write your paragraph again, without the mistakes.

2

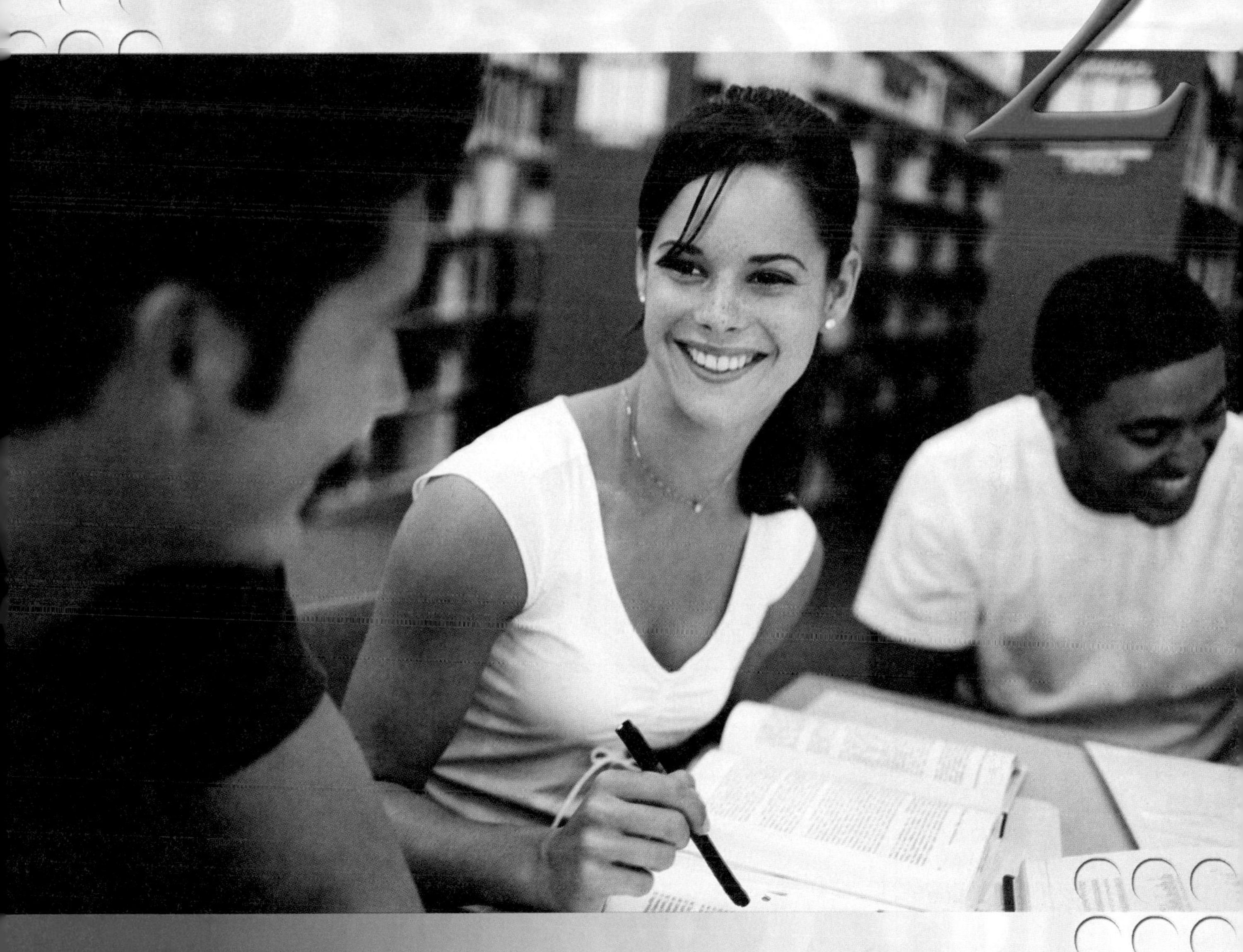

Language Learning

Discuss the questions.

- Look at the picture. Where are the people?
- Do you like to study with friends? Why or why not?
- What are the best ways to learn a new language?
- Read the chapter title. What do you think the chapter will be about?

PART 1 INTRODUCTION Emailing a Professor

BEFORE READING

THINKING AHEAD Answer these questions with a partner.

1. Sometimes a student is absent—not in class—for a day or a few days. What problems does this cause for the student?
2. If students are absent, what do they need to do?
3. Look at the four types of exams below.
   What type of exam is each one?
   Write the correct letter on the line under each exam.

Exam types

a. multiple-choice **b.** true/false **c.** essay **d.** short-answer

---

5. T F Both genes and education determine intelligence.

6. T F There isn't one "language center" in the brain.

7. T F It is better to learn words in groups than separately.

______

In 1-2 sentences, answer these questions:

1. Why are games (such as puzzles) a good way to learn something?
2. What are different kinds of memory?
3. What is the influence of the classroom on students?

______

---

9. Which part of the brain is important for language learning?

a. the cortex
b. Broca's area
c. Wernike's area
d. the angulat gyrus
e. all of the above

a

Write a short essay (1-3 paragraphs) to answer the question:

- What are the characteristics of the grammar-translation method?

______

READING

Read the emails. As you read, think about this question:

- What problem do Maria and Jennifer have?

From: "M. Aquino" <Maria_Aquino@earthlife.com>
Sent: Fri, 10 Nov. 2009 15:45:28
To: "Jennifer Klein" <jenny250@earthlife.com>
Subject: RE: Missed class

Hi Jen,

Sorry I didn't get back to you till now! I was absent, too, so I'm afraid I can't answer your questions. And I have some really, really bad news for both of us. According to Sara, there's an exam on Friday!!! ☹ We're gonna have to study FAST!

Okay, here's what I know: the exam is gonna cover all the stuff on the human brain from Chapters 7 & 8, and we need to know those different teaching methods from Chapter 9—you know, different ways to teach a foreign language. But one of us needs to email the prof. because maybe she assigned more. We need the class notes, too.

I'll email Dr. Snow if you get the notes from Sara, ok? Talk with you later. ☺

Maria

From: "M. Aquino" <Maria_Aquino@earthlife.com>
Sent: Fri, 10 Nov. 2009 16:11:57
To: "Professor Snow" <Drsnow@HSUF.edu>
Subject: Missed classes

Dear Dr. Snow,

I'm sorry to bother you, but I need a little help. Due to a family emergency, I was absent for the last two meetings of your 9:00 Education 251 class. Now I'm trying to prepare for the exam on Friday. Could you please answer two questions? 1) Will it be a multiple-choice test or an essay exam? 2) Is the exam going to cover only Chapters 7, 8, and 9, or will there be something else?

I appreciate your help.

Thank you,

Maria Aquino

30 From: “Amanda Snow” <Drsnow@HSUF.edu>
Sent: Sun, 12 Nov. 2009 9:32:45
To: “M. Aquino” <Maria_Aquino@earthlife.com>
Subject: RE: Missed classes
Hi Maria,
35 I'm glad you asked! It will be an essay exam, and yes, there are two more reading assignments. You need to read Chapters 4 and 11 in the other book, *Teaching with the Brain in Mind*. One chapter is on the influence of the classroom environment on students. The other chapter is about the role of memory in learning. They're very clear. I don't think you'll have a problem.
40 See you in class, Amanda Snow

AFTER READING

A. CHECK YOUR UNDERSTANDING Which sentences are true? Which sentences are false? Fill in (T) for True or (F) for False.

1. Both Maria and Jennifer were absent. (T) (F)
2. There is going to be an exam in two weeks. (T) (F)
3. The class is in biology. (T) (F)
4. Maria and Jennifer need class notes. (T) (F)
5. The students need to read chapters in two different books. (T) (F)

Reading Strategy

Understanding Tone

Some letters and emails are formal—proper, careful, and correct. Some are informal—casual and friendly—similar to the way people speak.

Informal	**Formal**
• used with friends	• used with people you don't know well
• used with peers	• used with managers, professors, and others to show respect
• sometimes uses incorrect spelling for the way words sound *(gonna)*	• uses correct spelling *(going to)*
• uses some informal words and slang *(stuff)*	• uses formal vocabulary *(family emergency)*
• can show emotion (☺)	• doesn't show emotion
• uses multiple punctuation marks *(???, !!!)*	• doesn't use unnecessary punctuation marks

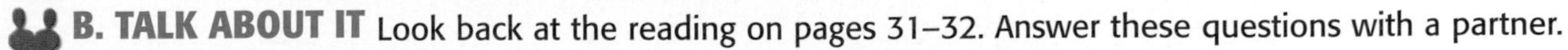

B. TALK ABOUT IT Look back at the reading on pages 31–32. Answer these questions with a partner.

1. Which email on pages 31–32 is the most formal? Why did the writer use a formal style?
2. Which email is the most informal? Why did the writer use this style?
3. Study the informal email. How do you know it is informal? How many characteristics of informal [illegible] you find?

PART  GENERAL INTEREST READING

The Brain, Learning, and Memory

BEFORE READING

A. THINKING AHEAD How does the brain learn and remember? Work in small groups to answer these questions.

1. In your opinion, what determines intelligence—genes or education?
2. Can the adult brain change and become better?
3. What things are easy for you to remember?
4. What things are difficult for you to remember?

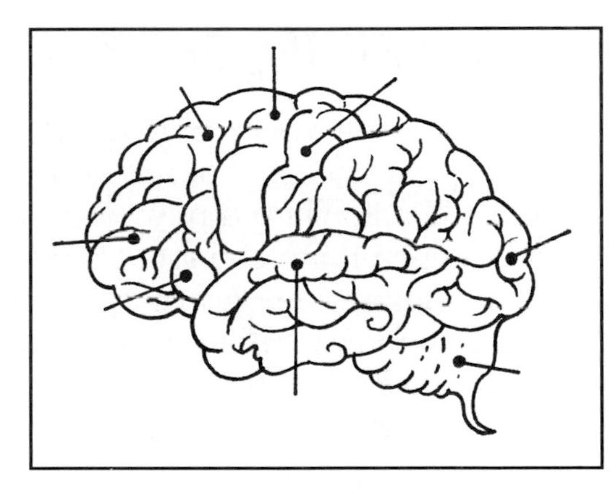

The human brain

B. VOCABULARY PREPARATION Read the sentences below. The words in blue are from the next reading. Circle the meanings of the words in the sentences.

1. For a few years, one educational method is popular. Then a new **approach**—(method)—appears, and everything changes.
2. In the right environment, **neurons**—brain cells—grow new connections.
3. Brain cells need **stimulation**—something new to experience.
4. The stimulation needs to be **challenging**—difficult, but not too difficult.
5. Is it important to find a **solution**—an answer to the problem?
6. A **mnemonic** is a technique to help the memory.

Reading Strategy

Guessing the Meanings of New Words: Examples

You don't always need a dictionary to guess the meaning of a new word. Sometimes you can know the meaning of the word from an example. Look after the words *such as* or *for example*.

Example: It's important to have **stimulation** **such as** a new movie, a new friend, a new place—anything new.

C. GUESSING THE MEANINGS OF NEW WORDS: EXAMPLES As you read, use examples to help you learn the meanings of some new words.

READING

Read this book review—a combination of an opinion and summary of a book. As you read, think about this question:

- According to the book *Teaching With the Brain in Mind,* how can we learn and remember things well?

The Brain, Learning, and Memory

New ways of teaching come and go. For a few years, one educational method is popular, and many teachers use it. Then a new approach—method—appears, and everything changes. So which ways are best? How can students learn fast and well? A new book looks at the human brain to answer these questions. Eric Jensen's *Teaching with the Brain in Mind* is an important book for any serious, creative reader.

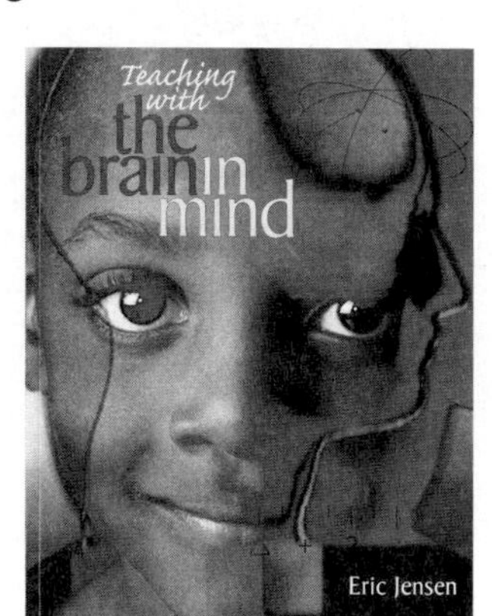

Teaching with the Brain in Mind, by Eric Jensen

Learning and the Brain

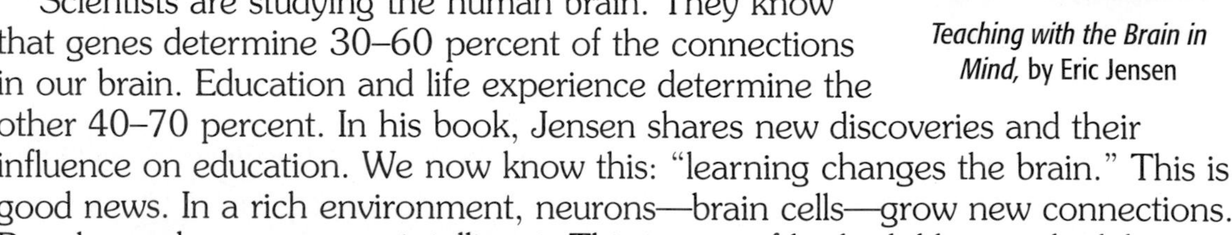

Scientists are studying the human brain. They know that genes determine 30–60 percent of the connections in our brain. Education and life experience determine the other 40–70 percent. In his book, Jensen shares new discoveries and their influence on education. We now know this: "learning changes the brain." This is good news. In a rich environment, neurons—brain cells—grow new connections. People can become more intelligent. This is true of both children and adults.

What is a "Rich" Environment?

The main characteristic of a rich environment is stimulation—something new to experience such as a new movie, a new friend, new information, a new place—anything. The stimulation needs to be challenging—difficult, but not too difficult. With too little stimulation, students lose interest. They become bored. With too much stimulation, students give up—stop trying.

According to Jensen, the "best way to grow a better brain" is to have the challenge of a new problem to work on. In a classroom, there are problem-solving exercises to work on such as word games, puzzles, discussions, or real problems. It isn't important to the brain to find a solution—an answer to the problem. Neurons grow because the brain is *working to solve the problem*, not because the solution is right or wrong.

A brain cell

The Brain and Memory

Many people say, "I have a bad memory. I can't remember people's names or words in a new language." In *Teaching with the Brain in Mind*, Jensen discusses different types of memory. One type is "linguistic memory" of words, names, numbers, and textbook information. Our new understanding of the brain tells us this about linguistic memory: "We remember best in chunks," not bits. "Chunks" are bigger than bits. For example, a chunk is a group of words, a sentence, or a song. A bit is one letter, one word, or one note of music. One way to remember information in chunks is with mnemonics. A mnemonic is a technique to help the memory. Mnemonics are helpful because they are chunks.

Common Mnemonics

To Help in Remembering		Mnemonic
• The colors of the spectrum, in order: **r**ed, **o**range, **y**ellow, **g**reen, **b**lue, **i**ndigo, **v**iolet	→	Roy G. Biv (a man's name)
• The planets, in order from the sun: **M**ercury, **V**enus, **E**arth, **M**ars, **J**upiter, **S**aturn, **U**ranus, **N**eptune, **P**luto	→	**M**y **v**ery **e**ducated **m**other **j**ust **s**ent **u**s **n**ine **p**encils.
• The spelling of some words: mov**ie**, p**ie**ce, rec**ei**ve	→	*I* before *E* except after *C*

Another type of memory is "body learning." This kind of memory lasts a very long time. For example, most adults can still remember how to ride a bicycle many years after they first learned. There is a connection between memory and physical actions such as sports, dance, or simply moving around the classroom. The brain and body remember together.

Eric Jensen's excellent book is important reading for both new teachers and experienced teachers. It is also good for students with a mind open to new discoveries about the brain, learning, and memory.

AFTER READING

A. MAIN IDEA What is the main idea of the reading? Fill in the correct bubble.

Ⓐ A new book is about the human brain.

Ⓑ A new book looks at new discoveries about the brain and their influence on education.

Ⓒ A new book discusses kinds of memory.

Reading Strategy

Using Graphic Organizers

A graphic organizer can help you visualize ("see") the main ideas and the details—the small ideas—in a reading. It can also help you visualize connections between ideas. One type of graphic organizer is the tree diagram below.

B. FINDING DETAILS To answer these questions, fill in the two tree diagrams.

1. According to the second paragraph (lines 9–15), what determines the connections in the brain?

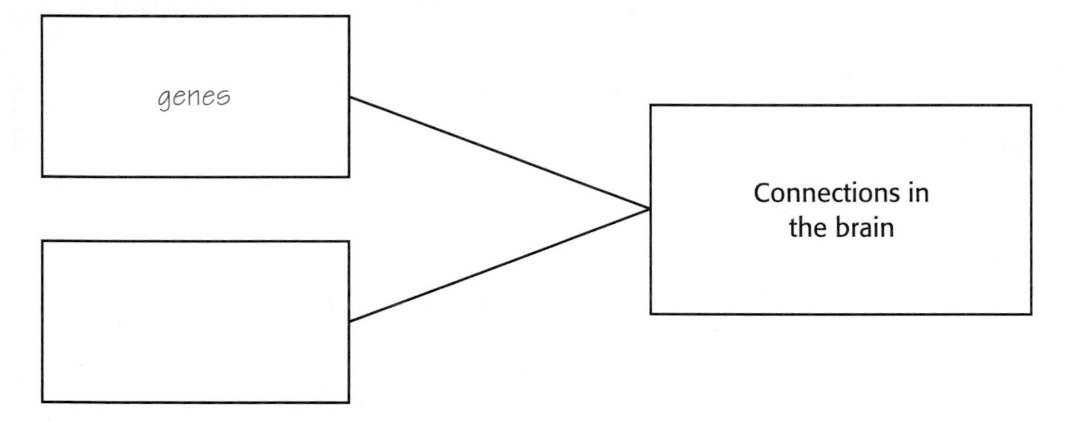

2. According to the fifth and sixth paragraphs (lines 30–54), what are two kinds of memory?

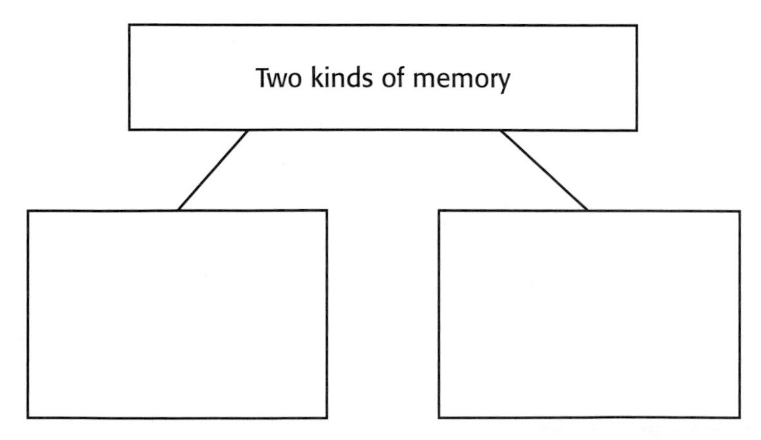

C. VOCABULARY CHECK Fill in the chart with examples from the reading on pages 34–35.

Word or Phrase	Examples
problem-solving exercises	word games
chunks	
bits	
physical actions	

D. APPLICATION How can the new discoveries about the brain help *you* be a better student? Discuss these questions in small groups.

1. If you want your neurons to grow new connections, you need stimulation. What kinds of stimulation can you bring into your life?
2. In his book *Teaching With the Brain in Mind,* Eric Jensen says the best way to grow a better brain is to have challenging problems to solve. In your English class, what problem-solving exercises do you do?
3. How can you better remember new words?
4. How can you use "body learning" to help you remember information?

PART 3 ACADEMIC READING

Methods of Learning a New Language

BEFORE READING

The grammar-translation method

Total Physical Response (TPR)

A communicative activity

A. THINKING AHEAD The reading on pages 39–40 is about different ways to learn a language in language classes. Think about your experience in this English class or other language classes. Discuss these questions in small groups.

1. Look at the pictures. Which one looks most like your English class? Explain your answer.
2. What activities do you know about that help you:
   - learn new words?
   - practice listening?
   - learn grammar?
3. Do you like some activities in your English class more than others? Which ones do you like? Which ones don't you like? Why?

B. VOCABULARY PREPARATION Read the sentences below. The words in blue are from the next reading. Match the definitions on the right with the words in blue. Write the correct letters on the lines.

__d__ **1.** The students need to read one **passage** in the book and listen to another passage on audio.

______ **2.** They **memorize** lists of new words.

______ **3.** The teacher gives **commands** such as "Stand up" or "Open your book."

______ **4.** The students are very **active**. They move around the class and do things.

______ **5.** The students **focus on** vocabulary. They spend a lot of time on this.

______ **6.** These **strategies** are techniques to help students with new words.

a. ways or methods to do something well

b. pay close attention to

c. moving a lot

~~**d.**~~ piece of writing or speech

e. instructions

f. learn and remember exactly

Reading Strategy

Guessing the Meanings of New Words: Parentheses

You don't always need a dictionary to guess the meaning of a new word. Sometimes there is a definition of the new word in parentheses (...) after the word.

Example: Students need to learn strategies for **note-taking** (writing information about a reading or listening passage).

C. GUESSING THE MEANINGS OF NEW WORDS: PARENTHESES As you read, look for meanings in parentheses.

READING

Read one student's essay exam. As you read, think about this question:

- What are five methods of teaching (or learning) a new language?

Education 251 **Essay Exam** **Name:** Maria Aquino

In one paragraph each, give a definition of the following methods. Include details about what students do in a language class with each method.

1. the grammar-translation method
2. TPR
3. the lexical approach

4. the Natural Approach
5. the content-based approach

1. The grammar-translation method is a way to learn a new language by translating it. Students have a reading passage in the target language (the new language). They use a bilingual dictionary (in the target language and their own language) and a grammar book. With this method, they read and look up all new words in the dictionary. They check the grammar book for rules. In this way, they translate the reading passage from the target language into their own language. They learn vocabulary by memorizing lists of new words. They don't learn to listen or speak.

2. With TPR (Total Physical Response) the teacher gives commands such as "Stand up," "Sit down," or "Open your book." The students show that they understand by doing these actions. They respond (answer) physically (with their bodies). They stand up, sit down, open their books, or whatever the teacher says. They listen a lot. Then they begin to speak. They give commands to each other, and students respond physically. In a TPR class, students are very active. They move a lot.

3. In the lexical approach, students focus on vocabulary, but they don't memorize lists of words. Instead, they study words in phrases (combinations of words) such as focus on vocabulary or respond physically. Students learn to notice groups of words. For example, they notice the preposition on after the verb focus. In this way, students learn more than new words. They learn how to use them.

4. In the Natural Approach, students focus on communication. They read or listen to passages in the target language. Then they respond in writing or through discussion with other students. They learn vocabulary by reading a lot and by being very interested in the readings. With this approach, there are no exercises in grammar, vocabulary, or spelling. The teacher does not correct students' mistakes.

5. With the content-based approach, students study academic material (reading or listening passages on content such as business, biology, or history). This material is in the target language. Students learn the vocabulary and grammar necessary to the content. They learn new words by 1) seeing them in readings, 2) practicing them in exercises, and 3) using them in discussions. They also learn strategies. These strategies are techniques to help students with new words, note-taking, reading, writing, and so on. Students spend a lot of time in group discussions and with problem-solving.

AFTER READING

A. CHECK YOUR UNDERSTANDING What is the main point (idea) of each method? Match the methods with the main points. Write the letters of the correct answers on the lines.

Methods	**Main Points**
__c__ **1.** the grammar-translation method	**a.** communication
______ **2.** TPR	**b.** academic content and strategies
______ **3.** the lexical approach	**c.** translating reading passages
______ **4.** the Natural Approach	**d.** following and giving commands
______ **5.** the content-based approach	**e.** vocabulary in groups of words

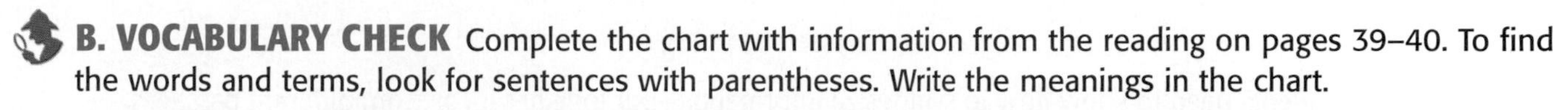

B. VOCABULARY CHECK Complete the chart with information from the reading on pages 39–40. To find the words and terms, look for sentences with parentheses. Write the meanings in the chart.

Word or Term	Meaning
target language	the new language
bilingual dictionary	
respond	
physically	
phrases	
academic material	

C. APPLICATION Look at this list. Which of these activities do you do in your English class? Check (✓) them. Then, in small groups, discuss this question: Which of these methods and techniques do you like?

_______ use a bilingual dictionary
_______ use a grammar book
_______ memorize lists of words
_______ move around the classroom
_______ study words in phrases
_______ translate from English to my language
_______ follow commands from the teacher
_______ notice phrases when I read
_______ read passages in English
_______ do grammar exercises
_______ learn strategies
_______ do vocabulary exercises
_______ read passages with new information
_______ discuss reading material with other students

Critical Thinking Strategy

Synthesizing

College students need to know how to synthesize information—put together ideas from different passages. Synthesizing is an important problem-solving skill.

D. PRACTICE: SYNTHESIZING The reading on pages 34–35 is about how the brain learns and remembers. The reading on pages 39–40 is about language-learning methods. Synthesize the information in small groups. Which learning methods make good use of different facts about the brain? Write the learning methods in the chart. Some learning methods can go in more than one box

Facts about the Brain	Methods
The brain needs a rich environment. The main characteristic of a rich environment is stimulation.	the Natural Approach
"The best way to grow a better brain" is to do problem-solving.	
"We remember best in chunks," not bits.	
The brain and body remember together.	

E. JOURNAL WRITING Choose *one* of these topics:

- something I learned about the brain
- something I learned about a good way to learn a language
- my favorite learning technique in my English class

Write about this topic for five minutes. Don't worry about grammar. Don't use a dictionary.

PART  THE MECHANICS OF WRITING

In Part 5, you will write about one way to learn a new language. You will need to use prepositions and one of these words: *or, but,* or *because*. Part 4 will help you learn how to use these.

Using the Word *Or*

The word *or* can mean "and" when you combine two **negative** ideas.

Example: I don't read Swedish. + I don't write Swedish. = I don't read **or** write Swedish.

A. PRACTICE: USING THE WORD *OR* On a separate piece of paper, combine these sentences with *or*.

1. I don't know Maria. I don't know Jen. I don't know Maria or Jen.
2. David didn't make mistakes in grammar. He didn't make mistakes in spelling.
3. We don't need to read Chapter 5. We don't need to read Chapter 6.
4. In that class, they don't practice listening. They don't practice speaking.
5. Julia doesn't have the class notes. She doesn't know the assignment.

Punctuation with the Word *But*

Use the word *but* to show opposite ideas. Use a comma before *but* when a subject and a verb follow it. Do not use a comma before *but* when there is not a subject and verb following it.

Examples: Most students like this exercise, **but they don't like** that one. — comma before *but*

Most students like this exercise **but** not the one on page 4. — no comma

B. PRACTICE: PUNCTUATION WITH THE WORD *BUT* On a separate piece of paper, combine these sentences. Use the word *but* in each combination.

1. I studied French. I didn't study Greek.
2. We worked on vocabulary. We didn't work on grammar.
3. Emma did Chapter 5. She didn't do Chapter 6.

4. We don't practice listening or speaking. That isn't a problem for me.

5. Some students think this is a problem. I don't.

Words in Phrases: Words after Prepositions

After most prepositions, there is a noun or **gerund** (a noun with *–ing*).

Examples: The lexical approach is a good method **of education**. (noun after *of*)
The content-based approach is a good method **of learning** English. (gerund after *of*)

Exception: Usually, after the preposition *to*, there is the simple form of the verb.

Example: I need **to solve** this problem.

To comes after these verbs: *need, want, hope, have* (= must)

The preposition *by* + a gerund answers questions with *how.*

Example: She found out about the exam **by asking** her classmate.

C. PRACTICE: WORDS AFTER PREPOSITIONS Fill in the blanks. Use a gerund or the simple form of the verbs in parentheses.

1. In the lexical approach, students focus on ____learning____ (learn) vocabulary.
2. In the Natural Approach, they don't worry about ________________ (have) correct grammar or spelling.
3. Most students think it's important to ________________ (practice) speaking.
4. On an essay exam, you need to ________________ (synthesize) information.
5. I'm interested in ________________ (learn) more about this.
6. He read Jensen's book to ________________ (learn) about the brain.
7. They're learning strategies for ________________ (read) well.
8. They respond in ________________ (write).
9. The stimulation needs to ________________ (be) challenging.
10. I hope to ________________ (do) well on the exam.

D. PRACTICE: ANSWERING QUESTIONS WITH *HOW* Answer the questions. Use *by* + the gerund form of the verb phrases in parentheses. (You can look back at pages 39–40 if necessary.)

1. In the grammar-translation method, how do students learn a new language? (translate it)
   They learn a new language by translating it.
2. In the grammar-translation method, how do students learn vocabulary? (memorize lists of new words)
   ____

3. In TPR, how do students show that they understand the teacher? (follow commands)

4. In the Natural Approach, how do students learn vocabulary? (read a lot)

5. In the content-based approach, how do students learn new words? (read them, practice them, and use them in discussion)

Using the Word *Because*

Combine two sentences with the word *because* to answer questions with *why*. Use the question as the first part of the answer. The word *because* is in the middle of the sentence. Don't use a comma.

Example: The students are taking the class **because** they need to learn the language.

E. PRACTICE: USING THE WORD *BECAUSE* Answer each question. Use *because* in each answer.

1. Choose a learning method that you like from pages 39–40. Why do you like it?

2. Choose a learning method that you don't like from pages 39–40. Why don't you like it?

F. REVIEW: EDITING A PARAGRAPH There are eight mistakes in this paragraph. They are mistakes with punctuation, prepositions, and parts of speech (gerunds and simple forms of verbs.) Find and correct them.

I think a good way to learning a new language is by use a combination of methods. Because there is something good about each one. For example, I like the idea of focus on communication in the Natural Approach but I like the lexical approach, too. Also, I need study academic material, because I hope go to college. That's why the content-based method is good.

PART 5 ACADEMIC WRITING

WRITING ASSIGNMENT

In Part 5, you will write one paragraph to answer this question:

• In your opinion, what is a good way to learn a new language?

MODEL

Here is a model of one student's work. First, just read the model. Don't write anything yet. You will follow these same steps beginning on page 48.

STEP A. CHOOSING A TOPIC Choose one language (English or any other). Check (✓) one of the five methods from the reading on pages 39–40.

Language: Latin

- [x] grammar-translation
- [ ] TPR
- [ ] the lexical approach
- [ ] the Natural Approach
- [ ] the content-based approach

STEP B. GETTING IDEAS Answer these questions. Write only short notes.

1. Which discovery about the brain supports your opinion? problem-solving

2. How does this method make good use of the brain? challenging translations, like puzzles

3. How do students learn by using this method? grammar book, dictionary → translation

4. What is one possible problem with this method? no listening or speaking

5. What is your response to this possible problem? goal not listening or speaking, only reading

STEP C. WRITING COMPLETE SENTENCES Use your answers from Steps A and B. Write them in complete sentences. Don't worry about spelling or grammar mistakes. (**Note:** There are some mistakes in the model sentences below.)

- In your opinion, what is a good way to learn a new language?

I think the grammar-translation method is a good way to learning Latin.

- Write your notes from Step B as complete sentences.

1. According to Jensen, the human brain needs solve challenging problems.
2. In a grammar-translation class, students have the challenge of translate difficult reading passages. These are like puzzles.
3. Students learn the language by use a grammar book and a bilingual dictionary to translate passages.
4. Students don't have practice in listening and speaking.
5. That isn't a problem. The goal is only to read because nobody speaks Latin these days.

STEP D. WRITING YOUR PARAGRAPH On a separate piece of paper, copy your sentences from Step C. (You can combine two sentences if you want to.) Use paragraph form. Indent the first line. After each period, continue on the same line. Don't worry about mistakes.

I think the grammar-translation method is a good way to learning Latin. According to Jensen, the human brain needs solve challenging problems. In a grammar-translation class, students have the challenge of translate difficult reading passages. These are like puzzles. Students learn the language by use a grammar book and a bilingual dictionary to translate passages. They don't have practice in listening and speaking but that isn't a problem. The goal is only to read, because nobody speaks Latin these days.

STEP E. EDITING Read your paragraph and look for mistakes with:

- *or*
- *but*
- *because*
- words after prepositions

STEP F. REWRITING Write your paragraph again, without the mistakes.

I think the grammar-translation method is a good way to learn Latin. According to Jensen, the human brain needs to solve challenging problems. In a grammar-translation class, students have the challenge of translating difficult reading passages. These are like puzzles. Students learn the language by using a grammar book and a bilingual dictionary to translate passages. They don't have practice in listening or speaking, but that isn't a problem. The goal is only to read because nobody speaks Latin these days.

YOUR TURN

Now follow Steps A–F to write your own paragraph about this question:

- In your opinion, what is a good way to learn a new language?

STEP A. CHOOSING A TOPIC Choose one language (English or any other). Check (✓) one of the five methods from the reading on pages 39–40.

Language: ______________________________

☐ grammar-translation

☐ TPR

☐ the lexical approach

☐ the Natural Approach

☐ the content-based approach

Writing Strategy

Getting Ideas

You can get ideas for your paragraph from:

- reading passages
- discussion with other students

On many essay exams, you need to synthesize information from different passages.

For the writing assignment in this chapter, use your chart on page 42 (Practice D) for ideas.

STEP B. GETTING IDEAS Answer these questions. Write only short notes.

1. Which discovery about the brain supports your opinion?

____

2. How does this method make good use of the brain?

____

____

3. How do students learn by using this method?

____

____

4. What is one possible problem with this method?

____

____

5. What is your response to this possible problem?

____

____

STEP C. WRITING COMPLETE SENTENCES Use your answers from Steps A and B. Write them in complete sentences. Don't worry about spelling or grammar mistakes.

- In your opinion, what is a good way to learn a new language?

____

- Write your notes from Step B as complete sentences.

1. ____
____
2. ____
____
3. ____
____
4. ____
____
5. ____
____

STEP D. WRITING YOUR PARAGRAPH On a separate piece of paper, copy your sentences from Step C. (You can combine two sentences if you want to.) Use paragraph form. Indent the first line. After each period, continue on the same line. Don't worry about mistakes.

STEP E. EDITING Read your paragraph and look for mistakes with:

- *or*
- *but*
- *because*
- words after prepositions

STEP F. REWRITING Write your paragraph again, without the mistakes.

UNIT 1 VOCABULARY WORKSHOP

Review vocabulary items you learned in Chapters 1 and 2.

A. MATCHING Match the definitions with the words. Write the correct letters on the lines.

Words	Definitions
__d__ **1.** passage	**a.** receive (from parents)
____ **2.** strategies	**b.** our idea of who we are
____ **3.** commands	**c.** fun
____ **4.** inherit	**d.** piece of writing or speech
____ **5.** identical	**e.** exactly the same
____ **6.** similar	**f.** anything
____ **7.** whatever	**g.** ways or methods to do something well
____ **8.** entertainment	**h.** almost the same
____ **9.** identity	**i.** clothes in a movie
____ **10.** costumes	**j.** orders

B. TRUE OR FALSE? Read the sentences below. Fill in (T) for *True* or (F) for *False*.

1. On a **multiple-choice exam**, you write a paragraph. (T) (F) [F filled in]
2. Albert Einstein was a **scientist**. (T) (F)
3. Non-identical twins have the same **genes**. (T) (F)
4. A **shy** person is a little afraid of other people. (T) (F)
5. A **setting** is a place. (T) (F)
6. A **puzzle** is physically difficult. (T) (F)
7. You think with your **brain**. (T) (F)
8. A **mnemonic** is a strategy to help you remember something. (T) (F)

C. WORDS IN PHRASES: PREPOSITIONS What prepositions can you put together with the words in blue? Fill in the blanks with prepositions from the box. Use some of the prepositions two times.

about	from	of	on	to

1. There's a big exam tomorrow, and we need to study. **According** _____to____ the professor, it'll be **different** __________ the last exam. This one will be a **combination** __________ multiple-choice and short answer. I think we need to **focus** __________ studying Chapter 2.

2. My Uncle Armen was a big **influence** __________ me. He was outgoing, and he told great **stories** __________ his favorite trips. He wasn't **afraid** __________ anything. I always wanted to be **similar** __________ him, but I don't think I am.

D. WHICH WORD DOESN'T BELONG? In each row, cross out the word without a connection to the other words.

1. height	~~emotion~~	weight
2. story	plot	role
3. techniques	methods	chunks
4. assign	respond	answer
5. upper class	middle class	English class
6. DNA	personality	genes
7. challenging	difficult	easy
8. material	short-answer	multiple-choice

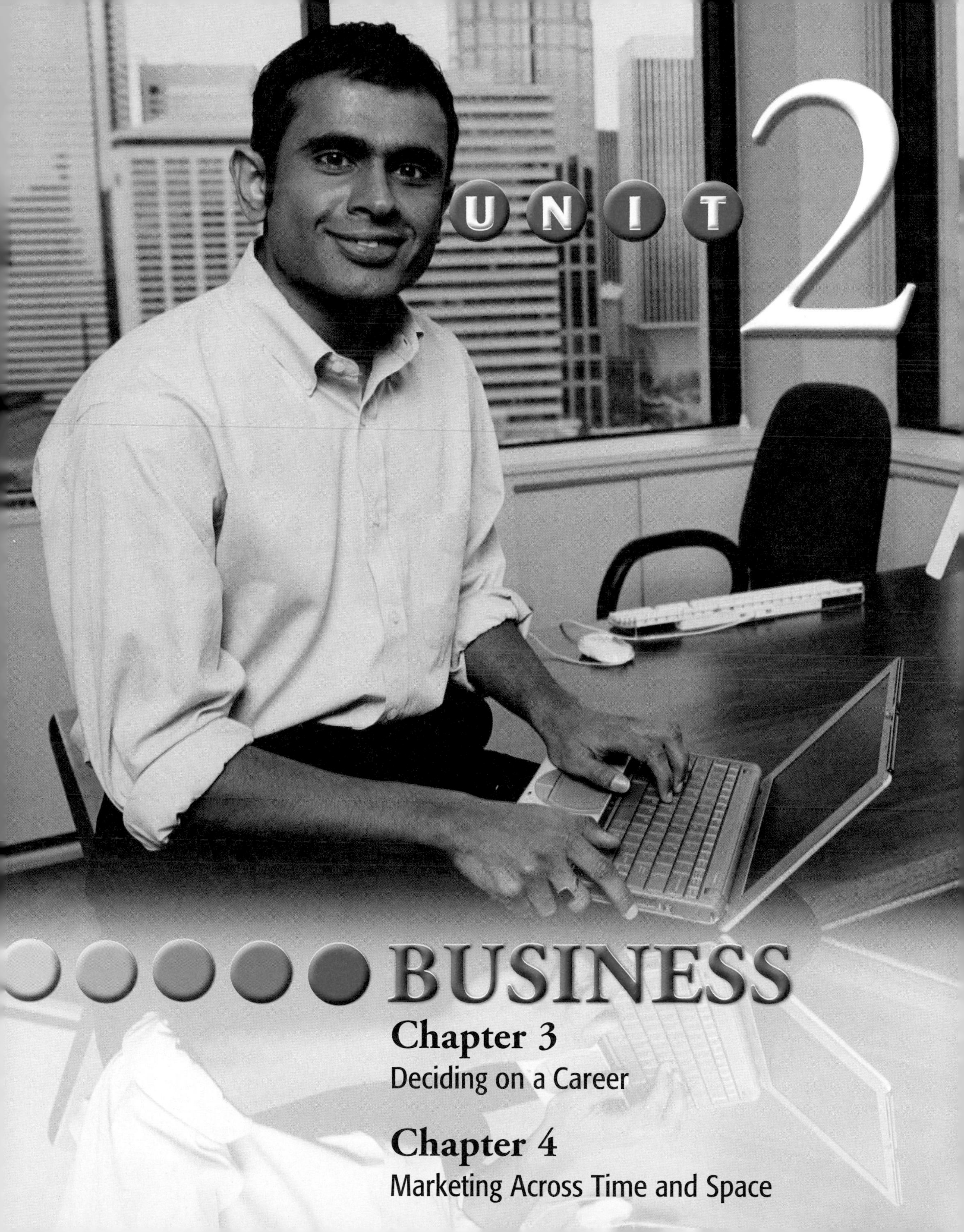

UNIT 2

BUSINESS

Chapter 3
Deciding on a Career

Chapter 4
Marketing Across Time and Space

CHAPTER 3

Deciding on a Career

Discuss the questions.

- Look at the picture. What is the young man doing?
- What are some good ways to look for a job?
- What is the best career for you?
- Read the chapter title. What do you think the chapter is about?

PART 1 INTRODUCTION Career Questionnaire

BEFORE READING

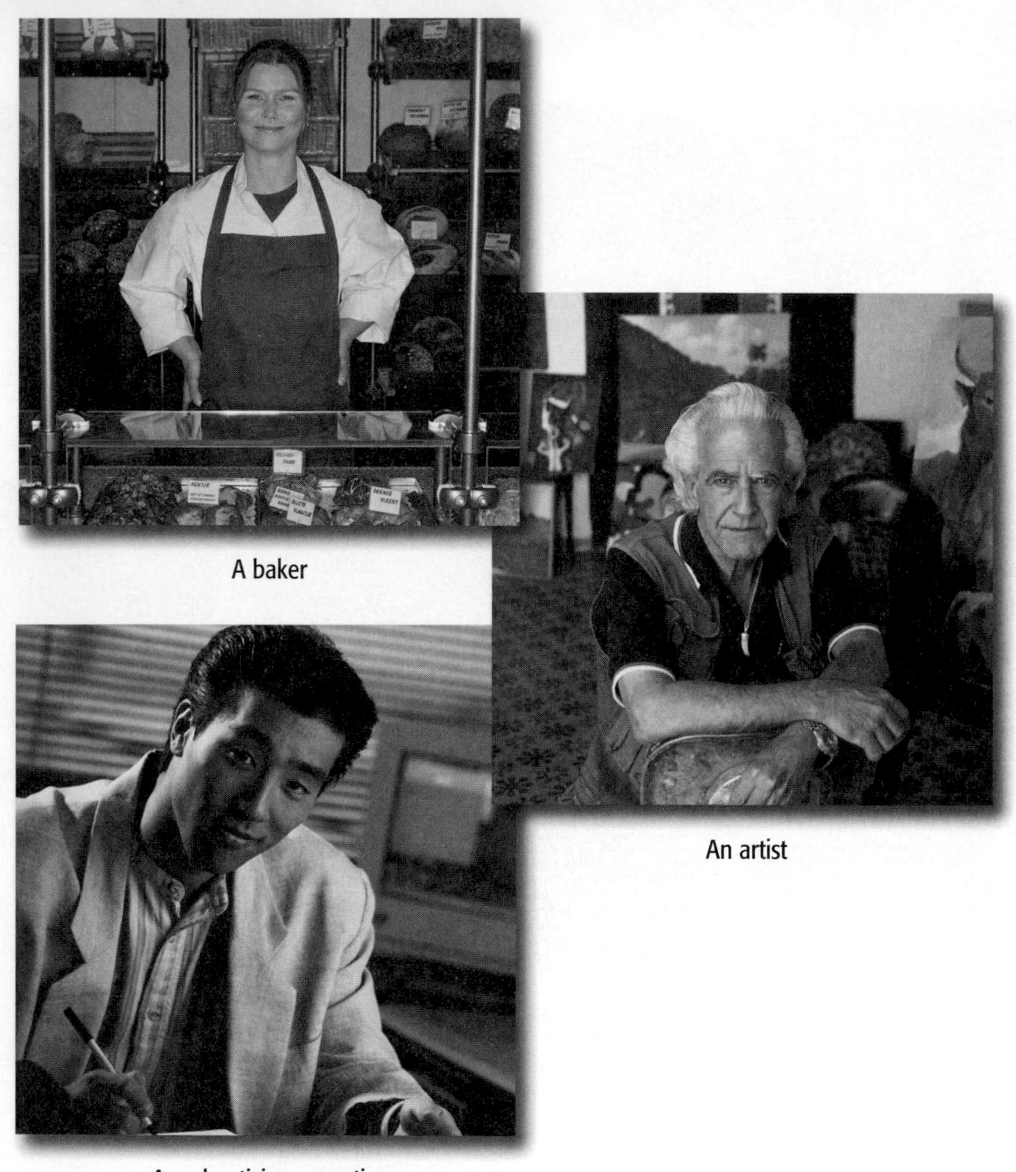

A baker

An artist

An advertising executive

THINKING AHEAD Answer these questions with a partner.

1. Why do people work—to make money, to help people, or for other reasons?
2. Do you have a job now? What is it? Do you enjoy it? Do you want to keep this job for many years?
3. Are you looking for a job? What kind of job are you looking for?
4. What kind of job do you want to have in five years?

READING

Read this questionnaire. Answer the questions about your likes, your dislikes, and things that you are good at.

Questionnaire

Part A

1. Check (✓) one or more boxes to complete these two sentences:
I like ______. I am good with ______.

Like	Am good with	
☐	☐	animals
☐	☐	ideas
☐	☐	plants
☐	☐	machines
☐	☐	numbers
☐	☐	other: ________________

Example

Like	Am good with	
☑	☑	animals
☐	☐	ideas
☑	☐	other: people

2. Check (✓) one or more boxes to complete these two sentences:
I enjoy ______. I am good at ______.

Enjoy	Am good at	
☐	☐	problem solving
☐	☐	physical activity
☐	☐	building things
☐	☐	working outside
☐	☐	languages
☐	☐	using computers
☐	☐	helping people
☐	☐	music
☐	☐	art
☐	☐	other: ________________

3. Check (✓) one or more boxes to complete this sentence:
I am happy when I am ______.

Happy when	
☐	in a big office with many people
☐	in a small office with only a few people
☐	at home
☐	outdoors (in a park, at a beach, in the mountains)

Happy when

☐ at school
☐ in a library
☐ in a hospital
35 ☐ in an art studio
☐ other: ____________________

Part B

Now write answers to these questions:

4. What are your five favorite **activities** (sports, hobbies, kinds of work—anything
40 that you like to do)?

____________________ ____________________

____________________ ____________________

____

5. What are (or were) your favorite classes in school? List one or more.

45 ____________________ ____________________

____________________ ____________________

____

6. What five activities or classes do (or did) you *not* like?

____________________ ____________________

50 ____________________ ____________________

____

AFTER READING

A. EXTENSION Use your questionnaire to write 5–10 true sentences on a separate piece of paper.

Examples: I like numbers.
I'm good with numbers.
I'm good at using computers.
One of my favorite classes in school is math.

B. TALK ABOUT IT Share your sentences in small groups. Talk about what kinds of jobs might be good for each person.

Example: You like numbers, and you're good with them. You're good at using computers. One of your favorite classes is math. You might be a good math or computer teacher.

PART 2 GENERAL INTEREST READING
Where Am I, and Where Am I Going?

BEFORE READING

A. THINKING AHEAD What things are important to understand about work? Answer these questions with a partner.

1. In your opinion, are most people happy with their jobs? Do they want to be doing something else?
2. At what age do people need to choose a **career**—their type of work?
3. Is it possible to change careers at the age of 30, 40, 50, or 60?
4. Do most people want **wealth**—a lot of money—from their jobs?
5. Do you know anyone in these situations?
   - going to begin college soon
   - **crazy about** (loves) one main subject
   - interested in many different subjects
   - in a career and is crazy about it
   - in a career and hates it
   - thinking about changing to a different **profession**—kind of work
6. Where are *you* in life? (See the choices in #5 for ideas.)

B. VOCABULARY PREPARATION Read the sentences below and on the next page. The words in blue are from the next reading. Match the definitions in the box with the words in blue. Write the correct letters on the lines.

> **a.** from a very long time ago
> **b.** It's too bad, but . . .
> **c.** notices on TV or the radio to sell something
> **d.** opinions to help someone
> **e.** person who can give good opinions
> ~~**f.**~~ the science of the way the brain works

__f__ **1.** I'm interested in the brain and how people think, so maybe I'll study **psychology**.

_____ **2.** I'm crazy about movies and the theater. I want to be an actress. **Unfortunately**, I'm really shy and not very outgoing.

_______ **3.** This is a good TV program, but there are too many **commercials**. I don't want to buy a car or lose weight!

_______ **4.** Lina took a class in **ancient** history—history from 2,000 to 4,000 years ago.

_______ **5.** Can you give me some **advice**—your opinion—to help me choose a career?

_______ **6.** I need some suggestions on college classes, so I'm going to ask the **counselor** for help.

Reading Strategy

Guessing the Meanings of New Words: Commas

You don't always need a dictionary to guess the meaning of a new word. Sometimes the meaning comes after a comma.

Example: I need to choose a **major,** (my main subject.)

C. GUESSING THE MEANINGS OF NEW WORDS: COMMAS As you read, look for the meanings of new words after commas.

READING

Read these paragraphs by four people in different life situations. As you read, think about these questions:

- What decisions do they need to make?
- Which person seems very happy?

Where Am I, and Where Am I Going?

These days, I think a lot about my future. I'm going to start college next year, and I need to choose a major, my main subject. It's a big decision because college will be preparation for my career after college. Here's my problem: I want to do everything! I love art and music, but I'm crazy about science, too. For example, I'm really interested in the brain and how people think, so I might major in psychology. Now, in high school, I don't have time for many after-school activities, but I'm in the chess club. I really like chess because it's challenging and because I'm good at problem solving. Unfortunately, chess is not a major in college!

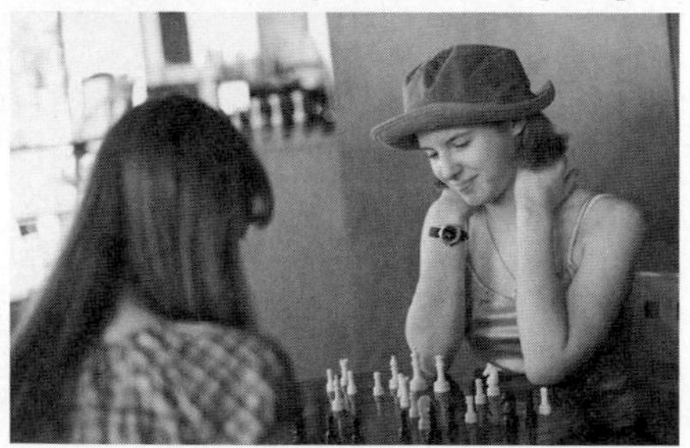

—Tiffany G.

I have the best job in the world, and I can't imagine doing anything else. I'm an archaeologist, a discoverer of people and places from the past. As a

15 child, I was crazy about ancient people—the Egyptians, Greeks, Romans, Mayas, Aztecs, and Incas. In college, I majored in archaeology. I have a great love for things from the distant past, from hundreds or thousands of years ago. Sometimes I find a piece of jewelry such as a ring or part of a necklace. I stand there with it in my hand, and I think, "I am the first person to hold 20 this in three thousand years." Sometimes I discover broken pieces of an ancient bowl. I carefully clean them and put the bowl back together. It's like a puzzle. I focus on it so hard that I forget everything else. I'm not aware of time and have no idea of the hour. I look up at the clock, and it's five hours later. It seemed like only minutes. Every day, I'm thankful for my work. It's 25 more than my profession. It's my life.

—Brian F.

I have a good job in advertising, designing and writing TV commercials to sell cars and other things. People seem to like my work. I'm good with words. I have an ability with words. And I work well with other people. The money is great. I have a big house, two cars, and a swimming pool. 30 My children are in expensive schools. We have a vacation house near the Pacific Ocean. However, I go to work every day and hate every minute of it. I don't like to sell cars. There isn't time to spend with my family or friends. There's a lot of money, but this wealth isn't making me 35 happy. I'm 42 years old and want to change my life. I dream about having my own business, maybe a small bookstore in a little town. Is this crazy? It's hard to give up everything and begin again. What should I do?

—Chris M.

I don't know what to do with my life. I'm in my first year of college, so I 40 need to decide on my major really soon. I hear advice from everyone. My father says, "You should become a doctor. Doctors make good money." However, I don't like medicine. My mother says, "You should major in education. You're good with children; you understand them and work well with them. Teachers always have a job, and there are lots of vacations." The 45 problem? I don't have a passion for teaching, no great love for it. The college counselor doesn't give this kind of advice. Instead, she looks at my grades in my classes and says, "You do very well in sports, business, and foreign languages. In these areas, you seem to have a real talent, a special ability." I like these three subjects. Should I major in physical education, business, or 50 Chinese? My Uncle Robert's advice is, "What do you love to do? Major in that. Don't worry about money. Money will come." Maybe he's right. I love to travel. I inherited this from him. Unfortunately, there isn't a major in traveling. What should I do?

—Diego C.

AFTER READING

A. CHECK YOUR UNDERSTANDING Read the sentences. Match the person's name with the correct situation. Write the correct letter on the line.

a. Tiffany G.	~~b.~~ Chris M.	c. Brian F.	d. Diego C.

__b__ **1.** This person is not happy at work and wants to find a new career.

_____ **2.** This person has many interests but needs to focus on one in college.

_____ **3.** This person is listening to advice to prepare for a career.

_____ **4.** This person is very happy with his or her career.

B. VOCABULARY CHECK Fill in the blanks with words and phrases from the box.

~~advertising~~	aware of	passion
archaeologist	the distant past	talent

1. I have a good job in ___advertising___, designing and writing TV commercials to sell things.

2. I'm a(n) ________________, a discoverer of lost people and places.

3. I have a great love for things from ________________, from hundreds or thousands of years ago.

4. I'm sorry I'm late. I was studying and wasn't ________________ the time passing.

5. I have a(n) ________________ for teaching, a great love for it. It's all I want to do for work.

6. In these areas, you seem to have a real ________________, a special ability.

C. MAKING CONNECTIONS: PARTS 1 AND 2 Choose one of the four people from the reading on pages 60-61. Imagine that you are this person. Go back to the career questionnaire on pages 57-58. How would the person from the reading fill out the questionnaire?

Critical Thinking Strategy

Thinking of Solutions

Giving advice is a type of problem solving task. When you give advice to another person, you need to think about his or her situation. Then you need to think of solutions that will help.

D. EXTENSION What advice can you give to Tiffany G., Chris M., and Diego C.? Work in small groups to give advice. Use *should* or *shouldn't* and the simple form of a verb in each answer.

Examples: Tiffany **should make** a list of all of her interests.
Tiffany **should find** professions to match her interests.
Tiffany **shouldn't worry** about the future.

PART 3 ACADEMIC READING The Joy of Work?

BEFORE READING

A. THINKING AHEAD Some people seem to have joy—great happiness—in their work. In your opinion, what are their secrets or special characteristics? Think about this question for a minute. Ask 10 classmates for their opinions. Write their answers on the chart.

Classmate	What is one secret (or characteristic) of people who love their work?
1	
2	
3	
4	
5	
6	
7	
8	
9	
10	

B. VOCABULARY PREPARATION Read the sentences below. The words in blue are from the next reading. Match the definitions in the box with the words in blue. Write the correct letters on the lines.

a. but
b. easily; without difficulty
c. get
d. includes
~~e.~~ not active
f. people who know a lot about something
g. sex (man or woman)

__e__ **1.** True happiness does not usually come from **passive** entertainment such as watching TV or sitting on a beach.

_____ **2.** Work **involves** *doing* something.

_____ **3.** Here are strategies from **experts**—people with special understanding of a topic.

_____ **4.** We can **acquire** understanding and information from experts.

_____ **5.** A river moves **smoothly** to the ocean.

_____ **6.** Some people love their jobs. **However**, many people are unhappy at work.

_____ **7.** A person's **gender**—male or female—doesn't determine happiness at work.

Reading Strategy

Guessing the Meanings of New Words: Finding Meaning in Another Part of the Sentence or in Another Sentence

You don't always need a dictionary to guess the meaning of a new word. Sometimes there is a definition of the new word in another part of the sentence or in the next sentence. Look around the new word for its meaning.

Example: They gave us **encouragement.** They said, "You can do it! Don't give up!"

C. GUESSING THE MEANINGS OF NEW WORDS As you read, look for meanings around the new words.

READING

Read about ways to be happy at work. As you read, think about this question:
• According to experts, what are the secrets of finding joy in your work?

The Joy of Work?

"When work is a pleasure, life is a joy!
When work is a duty, life is slavery."
—Maxim Gorky

Children often notice unhappy adults. They think, "Why do adults hate
5 their work? Why don't they choose *fun* jobs?" Look in any bookstore. There are hundreds of books on how to find happiness. Most of these books agree: true happiness does not usually come from passive entertainment such as watching TV or sitting on a beach. Instead, to experience true happiness, we usually must be active; we must be *doing* something. Surely, *work* involves
10 "*doing* something." Work is a big part of our lives. Most of us have to work. To be happy in life, we need to enjoy our work. So how can we choose the right type of work? Some people love their jobs. What can we learn from them? What are their secrets? Here are strategies from experts—people with a lot of knowledge of this topic.

Find the Right People

15 Who do you admire? Who are your heroes? These people are your role models. When you think of people you admire, you think, "I want to be like them." They can be members of your family, friends, neighbors, or teachers. They can be people from history or today's news. In *Secrets of People Who Love Their Work*, Janis Long Harris says, "They are the people who show us
20 how to dream." But we also need mentors, according to Harris. Mentors help or guide us. They give us encouragement: "You can do it! Don't give up."

Discover Your Talents, Passions, and Strengths

Everyone has certain talents—for running fast, singing well, solving puzzles, doing math problems. Genes seem to determine these abilities. Some people have certain talents, and some don't. We do not choose our talents. We can
25 choose only to use them or not. It's good to know our own talents because we often enjoy using them.

Our passions are feelings of great love for an activity. A person can have a passion for new languages, art, computers, animals, numbers, movies, traveling, science, sports—*anything*.

30 According to Martin E.P. Seligman, it's especially important to know our strengths. Everyone has certain strengths. We can choose to use them or not, like talents. How are they different from talents? In *Authentic Happiness*, Seligman explains that strengths are moral characteristics—abilities to know right and wrong and to choose right. We can *all* build on our strengths, and 35 we can all acquire new ones.

Examples of Some Strengths on Seligman's List:

- interest in the world
- social intelligence (the ability to notice people's emotions and respond to them)
- kindness
- honesty
- self-control
- the ability to work in a group
- gratitude (feeling or showing thanks)

40

Flow: What Is It?

Both Harris and Seligman write about the discoveries of Mihaly 45 Csikszentmihalyi. (Seligman helps us with the pronunciation: "cheeks sent me high.") This famous psychologist studies a wonderful condition. He calls it "flow." Most of us have experience with flow. Truly happy people experience it often.

To understand the word flow, think about a river. It moves smoothly and 50 easily down a mountain, through a forest, to the ocean. The river *flows* toward the ocean. A person sometimes experiences moments of flow in life.

These are times when an activity goes very smoothly and brings great happiness. Flow does not last long. It "visits you for a few minutes," as Seligman says. However, people who love their work experience it more often.

Who Experiences Flow?

55 In *Flow: The Psychology of Optimal Experience*, Csikszentmihalyi shares his discoveries. First, very different activities can produce "almost identical" feelings. For example, one person does something physically difficult such as climbing a mountain or swimming from France to England. Another person does something mentally difficult—plays a challenging game of chess or solves a 60 mathematics problem. Another person creates a piece of music. The activities are different, but all the people describe a similar experience of joy—great happiness—in their activity. And here is the second discovery: the person's culture, age, likes and dislikes, social class, and gender—male or female—don't matter. They aren't important. These characteristics don't seem to influence 65 the experience of flow. All people describe their experiences in a similar way.

The Characteristics of Flow

In an experience of flow, there is one of the following characteristics. Usually, there is a combination of several of them:

- **Challenge and Possibility** The activity must be both challenging and possible for the person to complete. It's a challenge for anyone to climb 70 a mountain or design costumes for a movie. However, these activities are also possible for people to do.
- **Focus** People have great focus during the activity. They don't think about anything else. A dancer thinks about only the movement. A reader focuses on only the story.
- 75 **Control** People have some feeling of control. They don't just follow directions from another person.
- **Sense of Time** During the activity, a person often experiences time differently. An hour can seem like a few minutes, or a few minutes can seem like an hour. The person loses all sense of time.

What Does This Mean to Me?

80 Over two thousand years ago, Aristotle asked, "What is the good life?" People with great jobs—artists, historians, and scientists, for example—seem to know the answer. They often experience flow in their work. So what can we learn from them? The experts agree. The secret seems to be this: find your talents, passions, and strengths. Then find work where you can use a 85 combination of them every day. What is your answer to Aristotle's question?

AFTER READING

A. CHECK YOUR UNDERSTANDING What are the secrets to finding happiness in our work? What do we need to find? Look at this list and check (✓) the correct answers.

_______ easy jobs

_______ people to give us advice and encouragement

_______ entertainment such as watching TV or sitting on a beach

_______ our talents

_______ our passions

_______ our strengths

B. VOCABULARY CHECK Look back at the reading on pages 65–67 to find the words and phrases in the box. Line numbers are given to help you find the words. Then match each word or phrase with its meaning. Write the word or phrase in the chart.

~~**admire**~~	**mentally**	**moments**	**role models**
don't matter	**mentors**	**moral characteristics**	

Line Number	Word or Phrase	Meaning
Line 15	admire	have a good opinion of
Lines 15–16		You want to be similar to these people.
Line 20		These people give you advice and encouragement.
Line 33		abilities to know right and wrong and to choose right
Line 51		short periods of time
Line 59		not physically; with the brain
Lines 63–64		aren't important

Reading Strategy

Understanding Pronoun References

Often, writers don't want to repeat a noun. In this case, they use a pronoun. Pronouns take the place of nouns. Some pronouns are *it, he, she,* and *they*. Look back before the pronoun to find its meaning.

Examples: Children often notice unhappy adults. **They** think, "Why do adults hate their work?" (*they = children*)

Visualize a river. **It** moves smoothly. (*it = river*)

C. PRACTICE: UNDERSTANDING PRONOUN REFERENCES What does each pronoun in the second sentence mean? Circle the noun in the first sentence. Then draw an arrow from the pronoun to the noun.

1. Why do adults hate their work? Why don't **they** choose fun jobs?
2. Mentors give us advice. **They** give us encouragement.
3. Everyone has certain strengths. How are **they** different from talents?
4. This psychologist studies a wonderful condition. **He** calls **it** "flow."
5. Flow does not last long. **It** "visits you for a few minutes."

Reading Strategy

Understanding Punctuation: Italics and Quotation Marks

Writers use italics for the title of a book. They use quotation marks for a person's words.

Example: In ***Secrets of People Who Love Their Work***, Janis Long Harris says role models are **"people who show us how to dream."**

Writers also use italics to emphasize (stress) a word.

Example: Some people ***love*** their jobs.

D. PRACTICE: UNDERSTANDING PUNCTUATION: ITALICS AND QUOTATION MARKS Look back at the reading. Find and circle words in italics and words in quotation marks. Which are titles? Which are a person's words? Which words are there for emphasis?

Titles: ______________________________

____

Person's Words: ______________________________

____

Emphasis: ______________________________

____

E. REVIEW: SYNTHESIS Look back at the reading in Part 2 (pages 60–61). Which talents, passions, and strengths does each person have? Write them in the chart.

Person	Talents	Passions	Strengths
Tiffany G.	problem solving	art, music, science	problem solving
Chris M.			
Brian F.			
Diego C.			

Which person experiences flow? Which characteristics of flow does this person have?

F. JOURNAL WRITING Choose one of these topics:

- something I learned about the secrets of happiness in work
- my experience with flow
- where I am in life now

Write about this topic for five minutes. Don't worry about grammar. Don't use a dictionary.

PART 4 THE MECHANICS OF WRITING

In Part 5, you will write a paragraph about your idea of the perfect job. You will need to use the future tense, modals (*may*, *might*), the word *or*, and gerunds. You will need to use correct punctuation with the words *first*, *second*, *third*, and *however*. Also, you will need to write about professions. Part 4 will help you learn how to use these.

The Future Tense

Use the verb *be* + *going to* + the simple form of a verb for a future plan.

Examples: I'**m going to start** college next year.

She'**s going to major** in business.

Possibility: *May* and *Might*

Use *may* or *might* + the simple form of a verb for something possible in the future.

Examples: I **may study** psychology. (= Maybe I'll study psychology.)

He **might major** in medicine. (= Maybe he'll major in medicine.)

A. PRACTICE: THE FUTURE TENSE Use *be going to* and *may* or *might* to answer these questions about the future.

1. What two plans do you have for your future education?

____

____

2. What are two possibilities for your future career?

____

____

3. Talk with one classmate. What are two of his or her plans for the future?

____

____

Using the Word *Or*

Use the word *or* to express possibilities. Notice the punctuation in these sentences.

Examples:	I'm going to go to City College **or** the state university.	no comma
	I'm going to go to City College, **or** I might go to the state university.	comma before *or* (Notice: there is a subject and a verb after *or*.)

Meaning of both sentences: I'll go to one of these schools, but I don't know which one.

B. PRACTICE: PUNCTUATION WITH THE WORD *OR* What choices do you need to make about your education or career? Write two sentences. Use the word *or* in each sentence.

____

____

Using *Enjoy* and *Involve*

Use a noun or a gerund (*-ing*) after the verb *enjoy* or *involve*.

Examples: She **enjoys** chess. She **enjoys** playing chess.

Research **involves** discovery. Research **involves** *discovering* cures.

C. PRACTICE: USING *ENJOY* AND *INVOLVE* What do you enjoy about learning English? What does it involve? On a separate piece of paper, write your answers to these questions.

Adverbial Conjunctions

When you give more than one reason for something, you can give each one a number using an adverbial conjunction. Begin the sentence with an ordinal number. Put a comma after it.

Examples: I enjoy archaeology for two reasons. **First**, I love the distant past. **Second**, I enjoy solving puzzles.

1 = first	4 = fourth
2 = second	5 = fifth
3 = third	6 = sixth

You can use these numbers for a list of things to do, too.

The word *however* means "but." When you begin a sentence with *however*, put a comma after it.

Examples: We have a vacation house near the Pacific Ocean. **However**, we don't spend much time there.

D. PRACTICE: ADVERBIAL CONJUNCTIONS Fill in the blanks in this paragraph. Use ordinal numbers (for example, *First*) and the word *however*. Begin each word with a capital letter. Put a comma after the word.

I love teaching for several reasons. ______First,______ I enjoy working with students and with other teachers. ____________________ I like the challenge. ____________________ I enjoy making a difference in someone's life. ____________________ I don't like to correct hundreds of exams.

Words in Phrases: Words for Work

Here are some professions (or fields) and the name for people in them. Notice how to use these words.

Professions	**People**
advertising	advertising executive
archaeology	archaeologist
business	businessperson
computer programming	computer programmer
education	teacher
medicine	doctor
psychology	psychologist
travel	travel agent, tour guide

Examples: Her career is in **travel.** She is a **travel agent.**

He works in **computer programming**.

He works as a **computer programmer**.

E. PRACTICE: WORDS FOR WORK Think of three people—a friend, a classmate, and yourself. Write two sentences about each person's future plans. What field is each person going to work in? What is this person going to do?

Examples: Elena's career is going to be in **education**.

Elena is going to work as a **teacher**.

____

____

____

____

____

____

F. REVIEW: EDITING A PARAGRAPH There are seven mistakes in this paragraph. They are mistakes with the future tense, modals (*may, might*), the word *or*, gerunds, punctuation with the words *first, second, third,* and *however*, and words for professions. Find and correct them.

In the future, I ‸am going to work in computer programming, or business. First, I have to choose a college, second, I need to decide on a major. I'm not sure what to do. I enjoy to work with computers. However I also want to work in my father's company. What can I do? I might working as a computer programmer in my father's company!

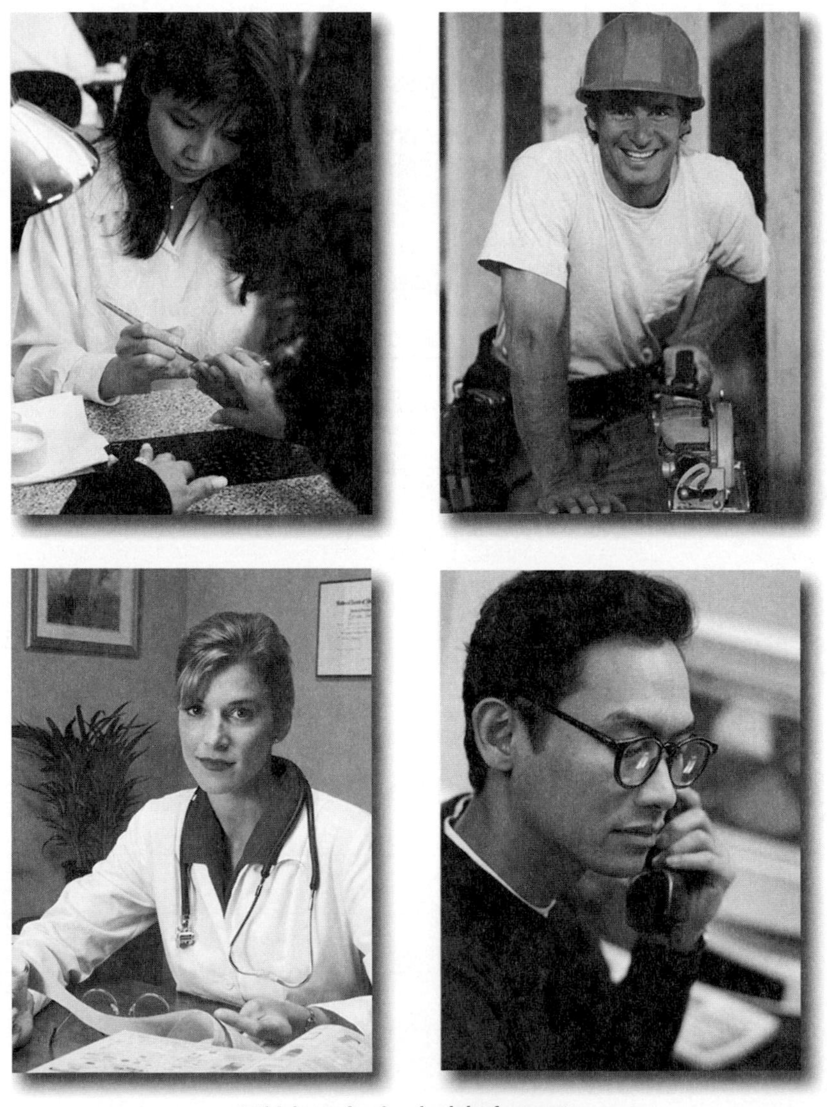

Which profession is right for you?

PART 5 ACADEMIC WRITING

WRITING ASSIGNMENT

In Part 5, you will write one paragraph to answer this question:
• What is your idea of the perfect career?

MODEL

Here is a model of one student's work. First, just read the model. Don't write anything yet. You will follow these same steps beginning on page 77.

STEP A. CHOOSING A TOPIC What is your idea of the perfect career? Check (✓) one. Write the career.

☐ your career now ______

☑ your future career medicine: doctor or pediatrician

STEP B. GETTING IDEAS Answer these questions about your perfect career. Write only short notes.

1. What is one reason for your choice? love biology and anatomy

2. What is another reason? enjoy helping people

3. What is a third reason? research, cures for diseases

4. What is one possible problem with your choice? medical school—hard!

5. What is your response to this possible problem? okay; ready for it

STEP C. WRITING COMPLETE SENTENCES Use your answers from Steps A and B. Write them in complete sentences. Don't worry about spelling and grammar mistakes. (**Note:** There are some mistakes in the model sentences below.)

• In what field is your perfect career?

My idea of the perfect career is in medicine.

• Write your notes from Step B in complete sentences.

1. I'm fascinated by biology and the science of anatomy, the way the human body works.

2. I enjoy to help people, especially children. Medicine involves changing people's lives in a positive way.

3. I love to do research. Research involves to discover cures for diseases. My research might making a big difference in the world.

4. Medical school is going to take many long, hard years.

5. I'm really ready for this challenge.

STEP D. WRITING YOUR PARAGRAPH On a separate piece of paper, copy your sentences from Step C. (You can combine two sentences if you want to.) Use paragraph form. Indent the first line. Add transition words such as *first, second, third,* and *however*. Use paragraph form. Don't worry about mistakes.

My idea of the perfect career is in medicine. I going to become a doctor or a pediatrician, a doctor for children, for three reasons, first. I'm fascinated by biology and the science of anatomy, the way the human body works. Second, I enjoy to help people, especially children. Medicine involves changing people's lives in a positive way. Third I love to do research. Research involves to discover cures for diseases. My research might making a big difference in the world. Medical school takes many long, hard years, however, I'm really ready for this challenge.

STEP E. EDITING Read your paragraph and look for mistakes with:

- tenses (present and future)
- modals (*may, might, should*)
- words for work
- *or*
- gerunds
- punctuation with *first, second, third,* and *however*

STEP F. REWRITING Write your paragraph again, without the mistakes.

My idea of the perfect career is in medicine. I'm going to become a doctor or a pediatrician, a doctor for children, for three reasons. First, I'm fascinated by biology and the science of anatomy, the way the human body works. Second, I enjoy helping people, especially children. Medicine involves changing people's lives in a positive way. Third, I love to do research. Research involves discovering cures for diseases. My research might make a big difference in the world. Medical school takes many long, hard years. However, I'm really ready for this challenge.

YOUR TURN

Now follow Steps A–F to write your own paragraph about this question:

- What is your idea of the perfect career?

STEP A. CHOOSING A TOPIC What is your idea of the perfect career? Check (✓) one. Write the career.

- ☐ your career now ______________________
- ☐ your future career ______________________

STEP B. GETTING IDEAS Answer these questions about your perfect career. Write only short notes.

1. What is one reason for your choice? ______________________

2. What is another reason? ______________________

3. What is a third reason? ______________________

4. What is one possible problem with your choice? ______________________

5. What is your response to this possible problem? ______________________

Writing Strategy

Writing Complete Sentences

Every sentence in a paragraph must be complete. A sentence must have a subject (a noun or phrase with a noun) and a verb.

Examples: **I love** to do research.
s v

My idea of the perfect career is in medicine.
s (noun phrase) v

Every sentence must begin with a capital letter. It must end with a period (.), question mark (?), or exclamation point (!).

Examples: **D**octors make good money**.**

What should I do**?**

I want to do everything**!**

Do not put two sentences together without a word such as *because* or a comma and a word such as *and* or *but*.

Examples: I'm going to start college, **and** I need to choose a major.

I love art and music, **but** I'm crazy about science, too.

I like chess **because** it's challenging.

STEP C. WRITING COMPLETE SENTENCES Use your answers from Steps A and B. Write them in complete sentences. Don't worry about spelling and grammar mistakes.

- In what field is your perfect career?

____

- Write your notes from Step B in complete sentences.

1. ____

____

____

2. ____

____

____

3. ____

____

____

4. ____

____

____

5. ____

____

____

STEP D. WRITING YOUR PARAGRAPH On a separate piece of paper, copy your sentences from Step C. (You can combine two sentences if you want to.) Use paragraph form. Indent the first line. Add transition words such as *first, second, third,* and *however*. Use paragraph form. Don't worry about mistakes.

STEP E. EDITING Read your paragraph and look for mistakes with:

- tenses (present and future)
- modals (*may, might, should*)
- words for work
- *or*
- gerunds
- punctuation with *first, second, third,* and *however*

STEP F. REWRITING Write your paragraph again, without the mistakes.

4

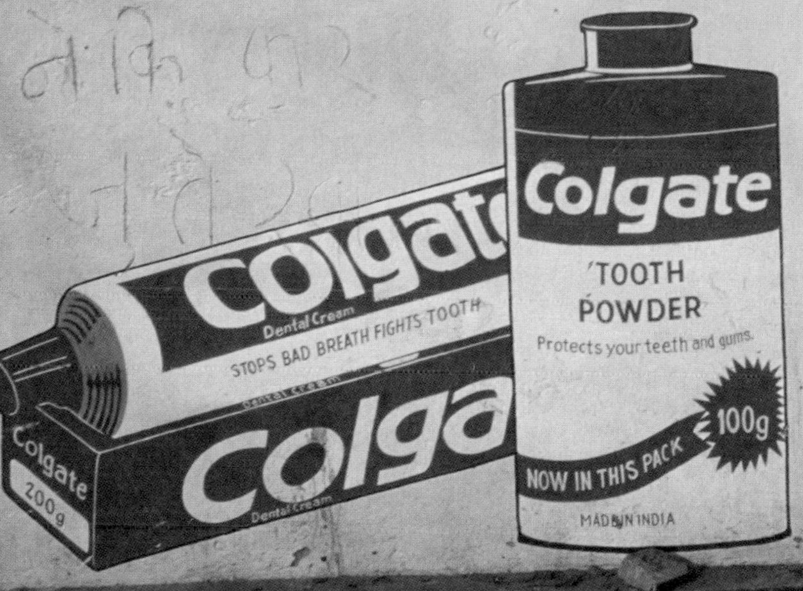

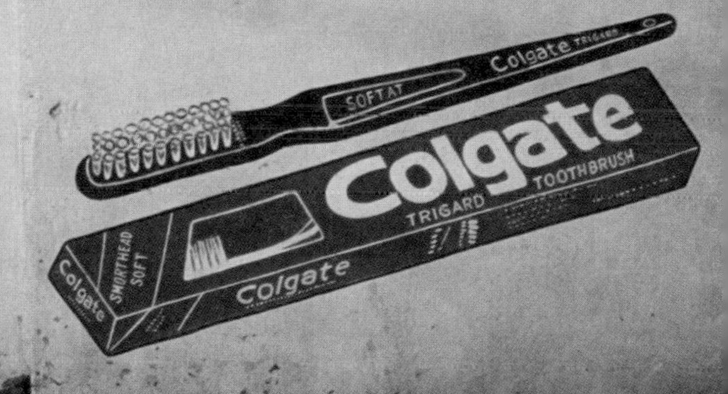

Marketing Across Time and Space

Discuss the questions.

- Look at the picture. What country is the billboard in?
- What is the billboard advertising?
- What are some of the most popular American products that are sold in other countries?
- Read the chapter title. What do you think the chapter will be about?

PART 1 INTRODUCTION Selling Movies

BEFORE READING

A woman enjoying a movie

THINKING AHEAD Look at the pictures on pages 83 and 95. Then answer these questions with a partner.

1. Do the movies look interesting to you? Why? Why not?
2. Name the last movie that you saw. Which country did it come from?
3. What is your favorite movie? Which country did it come from?
4. What type of movies do you like best? Why?

READING

Read about movie titles. As you read, think about this question:

- Movies sometimes have different titles in different countries. Why?

Same Movie, Different Name

People around the world enjoy movies from other countries. Movies from England, the United States, France, and Japan are especially popular. However, to "sell" a movie in a foreign country, movie studios often get a local company (in the foreign country) to give the movie a new title. Sometimes the local company translates the title of the movie for the new country. Sometimes the company creates a completely new title. It is often a challenge to choose a title. Let's look at some examples.

Often the new title of the movie is identical to the original one. An example is the American film *Along Came Polly*. In Germany, the title was *...und dann kam Polly*, a direct translation. However, sometimes the movie makers do not translate original titles directly. Instead, they make changes that "sound" good in the foreign language. For example, the American movie *You've Got Mail* was *Yū gatto mēru* in Japan. The new spelling of the words shows how the English title sounds to Japanese ears.

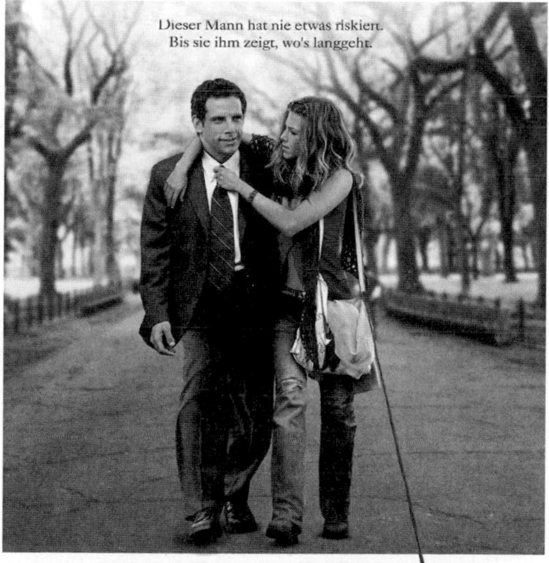

Along Came Polly English and German posters

Sometimes movie titles are completely different in another country. When the local companies change a title, they often try to communicate the main idea of the movie. For instance, in Japan, *Out of Africa* became *The End of Love and Sorrow*, and in China, *101 Dalmations* was *Big March of 101 Doggies*. In France, *Legally Blonde* was *A Blonde's Revenge*. This title clearly communicates the main idea of the movie. Sometimes local companies make mistakes. For example, the plot of the movie *As Good as It Gets* was about a romance between a writer and a waitress. In Japan, it became *A Romance Novel Writer*. (The mistake? The hero did not write romance novels.) In Taiwan, *Deep Impact*, a movie about an asteroid (a medium-sized rocky object) hitting the Earth, was *A Planet Will Hit the Earth*. (The mistake? A planet is not the same as an asteroid.) In these cases, the original title means one thing. The new title means something else.

Same Movie, Same Name

Sometimes there is no translation of a foreign movie title. For example, the Mexican movie *Amores Perros* and the Japanese movie *Tampopo* both kept their original titles in the United States. Sometimes the original title sounds good to foreign ears. The foreign name might help to sell the movie because it makes the movie sound more interesting.

AFTER READING

A. CHECK YOUR UNDERSTANDING Fill in (T) for True or (F) for False.

1. Movie titles are usually the same around the world. (T) (F)
2. *Yū gatto mēru* is an example of a movie title with a new spelling. (T) (F)
3. The German title of *Along Came Polly* is a direct translation of the English title. (T) (F)
4. The French title for *Legally Blonde* correctly expresses the main idea of the movie. (T) (F)
5. The Taiwanese title for *Deep Impact* was *An Asteroid Will Hit the Earth*. (T) (F)
6. The Japanese movie *Tampopo* had a different title in the United States. (T) (F)
7. Foreign titles sometimes help to sell movies. (T) (F)

 **B. TALK ABOUT IT** With a partner, write the titles of four movies that were not produced in English. Then directly translate two of the titles into English. Next, write new titles that communicate the main ideas of the other two movies.

Movie	Your Title	Type
Example: Invasión de los Vampiros	Invasion of the Vampires	direct translation
Example: Le Grand Bleu	The Ocean, My Love	new title
1.		
2.		
3.		
4.		

PART  GENERAL INTEREST READING
Advertising Through History

BEFORE READING

Billboard for a *Harry Potter* movie

Online commercial for BMW

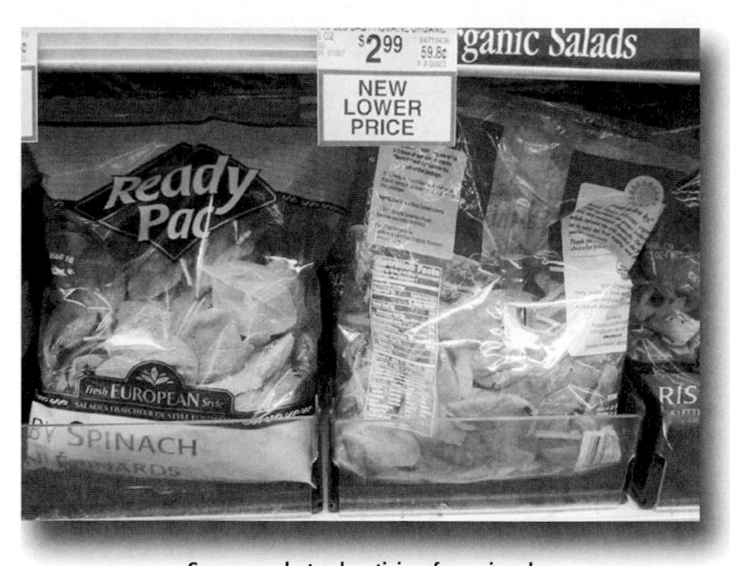

Supermarket advertising for spinach

A. THINKING AHEAD Look at these types of advertising. Discuss the answers to these questions in small groups.

1. Where are five places you see advertising?
2. What is your favorite advertisement? Why? What type of ad is it?

B. VOCABULARY PREPARATION Read the sentences below. The words in blue are from the next reading. Match the definitions in the box with the words in blue. Write the correct letters on the lines.

a. get the interest of	c. interesting points	f. show
b. group of people who buy something	d. making people angry	g. successful
	~~e.~~ money for working	h. very good quality

__e__ **1.** This product is for wealthy people, people with an **income** of about $100,000 a year.

_____ **2.** Katie bought a **high-performance** car. It goes smoothly at a very high speed.

_____ **3.** Advertisements in movie theaters are **irritating**. Most people don't like them.

_____ **4.** We learned lots of interesting things about advertising. One of the **highlights** was an ancient Chinese ad.

_____ **5.** Many ads **reflect,** or tell, important ideas that people have about life.

_____ **6.** This ad is really **effective**. People see it, and they want to buy the product.

_____ **7.** Most advertisers want to **attract** a certain group of people—the people who will buy the product.

_____ **8.** One group, older people with money, makes up the best **market** for jewelry advertisements.

Reading Strategy

Guessing the Meaning of New Words: Adjective Clauses with *Who* and *That*

Sometimes the definition of a word includes an adjective clause. The adjective clause often begins with *who* or *that*. The adjective clause gives more information about the noun that goes before it.

Example: Commercials are ads **that are on TV, radio, or the Internet.**

C. GUESSING THE MEANINGS OF NEW WORDS: ADJECTIVE CLAUSES WITH *WHO* AND *THAT* As you read, notice the meanings of words in adjective clauses with *who* or *that*.

READING

Read about advertising through history. As you read, think about this question:

- How is advertising in the past similar to advertising today?

Advertising Through History

Ads are everywhere: on TV and radio, on buses and buildings, even at soccer games. They can be funny, irritating, or informative. Advertising isn't new; archaeologists have found ads that are over 5,000 years old. Some of the oldest types of advertising are outdoor displays, signs with pictures and 5 words that describe a product or service. These are similar to billboards today. Many of these signs were used in ancient Rome more than 2,000 years ago.

In the Middle Ages (500 A.D.–1500 A.D.), word of mouth—talking about a product or service—was an effective form of advertising. Town criers were people who walked up and down streets and shouted out the qualities of items 10 for sale. This was the most common form of advertising in Europe. Then the printing press was invented in the 1400s. With it, advertisers printed many copies of ads. Because of the printing press, large numbers of people in many different places could receive ads. This made a big change in advertising in the Western world.

15 Now, there are even more ways and places to advertise products and services because of modern technology. Today, there are ads in movies and on the Internet. Here are some highlights of advertising throughout history.

Package Ads: China, 1271–1368

Papermaking and printing appeared early in China, a long time before they appeared in Europe. As a result, China probably had the first printed 20 advertisements. Recently, archaeologists in China found some 700-year-old printed-paper ads. They may be the first printed paper ads in the world. The ads are packaging: pieces of paper with writing on them that were wrapped around a paint product. The writing on them describes the paint and gives the address of the shop that made it. Like modern ads, the wrapping even has 25 promotional language (words that describe the good things about the product). For example, the writing says, "Compared with other paints, the color of our product is the best." It also has the company's trademark, a symbol representing the company.

Hikifuda: Japan, late 1800s

Hikifuda are Japanese handbills (printed cards or pieces of paper used for 30 advertising). *Hikifuda* advertised products and shops. Printers made them with woodblocks, pieces of wood with designs cut into them. *Hikifuda* have colorful pictures on the right side and space for writing on the left side. As in 35 some modern advertising, these pictures make the consumer (buyer) feel good about the product or shop. They reflect the values of 19th century Japanese consumers. These values are ideas about 40 life that people think are important such as luck, prosperity (wealth), or a connection to the past.

This hikifuda shows Ebisu, the god of prosperity.

Online Commercials: Worldwide, early 2000s

A modern type of advertising is the online commercial. In 2001, the auto maker BMW showed short online commercials to advertise the Z4 Roadster. 45 They appeared on the company website. Famous directors such as Ang Lee and Guy Ritchie made the films. They starred British actor Clive Owen in the role of "Mysterious Driver." In the commercials, the hero experiences a series of dangerous situations and handles them expertly thanks to his high-performing BMW. The online commercials were very successful. They helped BMW to 50 attract their target market, males who have an income of $75,000 or higher. These ads succeeded because they were creative, entertaining, and got people's attention.

AFTER READING

A. MAIN IDEA What is the main idea of the reading? Fill in the correct bubble.

Ⓐ The history of advertising began with billboards.

Ⓑ The history of advertising began in ancient times and continues in the modern world.

Ⓒ The history of advertising began in the modern world.

Reading Strategy

Making Notes

It's a good idea to make notes as you read. It helps you to focus on and remember important information. Here is one way to make notes as you read: Underline or circle important information such as dates, names, and numbers.

Example: Then the printing press was invented (in the 1400s.)

B. FINDING DETAILS Look back at the reading on pages 88-89. Find dates, places, and names of different types of advertising. Underline or circle them. Then match the types of advertising with the correct times and places below.

Times and Places	Types of Advertising
d 1. Japan, late 1800s	a. word of mouth
____ 2. Europe, Middle Ages	b. outdoor displays similar to billboards
____ 3. China, 1271-1368	c. package ads
____ 4. ancient Rome	~~d.~~ *hikifuda*

C. VOCABULARY CHECK Fill in the blanks with words or phrases from the box.

outdoor displays	town criers	~~values~~
packaging	trademark	

1. The ad reflected two important ____values____ in Thai culture: family and luck.
2. The paint product was covered with ________________. It showed the price and the company that made the paint.
3. There were no commercials in the Middle Ages. Instead, there were ________________, people who shouted about products in the streets.
4. Archaeologists discovered the first printed ________________, a paint company's symbol, on pieces of ancient Chinese paper.
5. ________________, signs with writing and pictures, are the oldest type of advertising.

Tag Heuer watches

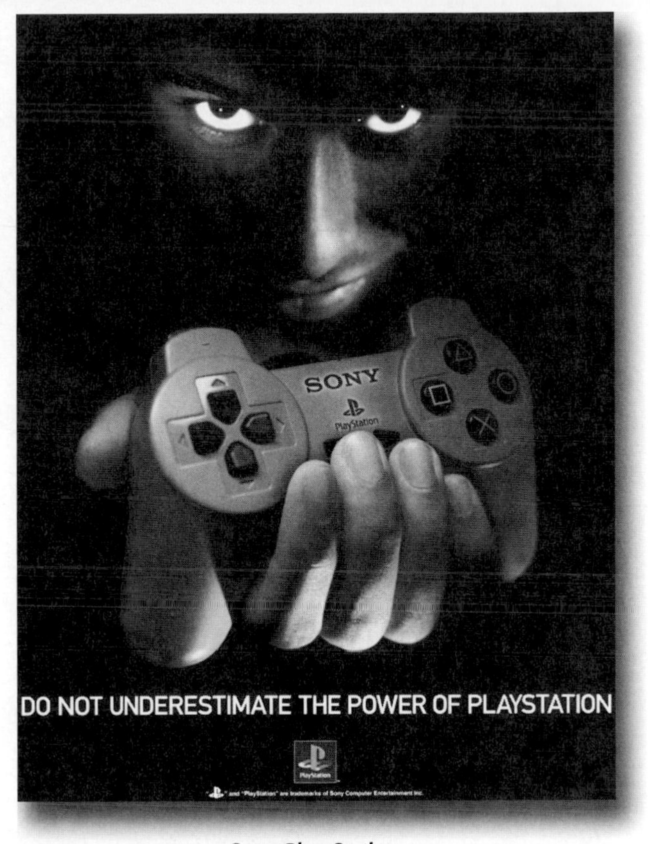

Sony Play Station

D. APPLICATION Look at these ads. For each one, work in small groups and discuss the questions below:

1. What kind of information do the ads include?
2. Does the product have a trademark? If yes, what does it look like?
3. What values do the ads reflect?
4. How do the ads get your attention?

PART 3 ACADEMIC READING Modern Advertising

BEFORE READING

A. THINKING AHEAD Ads are made for different kinds of people. Ads try to give people a feeling about a product. This feeling is called **product image**. In small groups, discuss the product image for each ad. What kinds of people will each ad appeal to?

B. VOCABULARY PREPARATION Read the sentences below. The words and phrases in blue are from the next reading. Match the definitions in the box with the words in blue. Write the correct letters on the lines.

a. be a part of	**e. particular**
b. calls attention to	**f. people who admire sports teams and players**
c. make better	**~~g.~~ something that has no use**
d. not going away	**h. using a computer mouse**

__g__ **1.** There is no use for this product; it's just **junk**.

______ **2.** The ad suggests, "If you want to **improve** your life, just buy this expensive car, and everything will be better."

______ **3.** Most people want to **belong to** a group because they want to feel popular.

______ **4.** April knows exactly which car she wants; she wants a **specific** one, the new BMW.

______ **5.** The Internet makes shopping easy. By **clicking a button**, you can buy almost anything.

______ **6.** This new car looks safe. The commercial for it **appeals to** the need for safety.

______ **7.** We will always have ads; they're **here to stay**.

______ **8.** Baseball **fans** pay a lot of money to see their favorite sport, and they don't want to see commercials at the ballpark.

Reading Strategy

Guessing the Meanings of New Words: Colons

You don't always need a dictionary to guess the meaning of a new word. Sometimes there is an example or explanation of the word after a colon(:).

Example: Advertising creates a product's **image:** a value that people connect with it.

C. GUESSING THE MEANINGS OF NEW WORDS: COLONS As you read, look for explanations of words after colons.

READING

Read about modern advertising. As you read, think about this question:
- How do advertisers reach consumers?

Modern Advertising

It's a fact of life: people who make products need to sell them. This was true in ancient times, and it's even truer today. The product might be beautiful, useful, or necessary. It might be useless junk. Either way, it must get from the maker to the consumer. Advertisers are always thinking of new ways to make this happen.

Advertising

5 Companies create products and services, give them prices, and then want to get them to consumers. To do this, advertising companies tell 10 consumers about the price or special qualities (characteristics) of theproducts or services. Successful advertising influences people to buy something. 15 It makespeople feel that the product or service will improve their lives. One strategy of advertisers is to appeal to people's emotional needs: the need for love, the need to belong to a group, to feel safe, to feel good about themselves, or to feel better than others. For example, advertisers will suggest 20 that a person who uses a certain shampoo will be popular. An ad for an SUV might target the need for safety in a dangerous world.

A sports utility vehicle (SUV)

Product Image

More importantly, advertising creates a product's image: the values that the consumer connects with it. The image might be youth, luxury, or energy. For example, advertisers might create an image of luxury for a certain type of car. 25 They might show an upper-class couple driving to a luxury hotel in the car. The consumer thinks, "If I buy this expensive car, it means that I have a luxurious lifestyle." Consumers frequently buy a product for its image even more than for its price or quality.

Types of Advertising

Advertisers reach consumers in many ways: through TV, newspapers, direct 30 mail, radio, magazines, the Internet, and outdoor advertising. They use different methods for different products. For example, they use TV commercials for common products such as food because TV commercials can tell a story. They use pictures, sound, and motion to create drama. Advertisers use Internet advertising when they want to personalize an advertisement. Through the Internet, advertisers can get information about users. Then they use that information to create specific advertising messages. Internet advertising is also direct; users can buy products immediately by clicking a button.

Product Placement

Another type of advertising is product placement. With product placement, a product appears in a TV show, a movie, a music video, a book, or a computer game. Often the product is placed in one or more scenes in a natural situation, but the actors never talk about it, especially in movies.

We all experience product placement. However, we don't always notice it. Here are some examples:

- Tommy Lee Jones and Will Smith wear RayBan sunglasses in *Men in Black*.
- Tom Hanks makes friends with a Wilson soccer ball in *Cast Away*.
- Elliot and ET eat Reese's Pieces in *ET*.
- In the computer game *Crazy Taxi*, customers ask to go to Pizza Hut.

Moviemakers, game designers, and TV production companies like to use real products because name brands—famous products—make a situation more realistic. For instance, if the star is holding a can of "Pepsi," it looks realistic. If she is holding a can that says "Soda," it doesn't look realistic.

Advertisers like product placement, too. It is an inexpensive way to have millions of people see their products. Suzanne Forlenza is responsible for product placement at Apple Computer. She says, "By putting one PowerBook in a movie like *Mission Impossible*, you get your product shown in every country in the world . . . for the cost of loaning the product."

Companies are always looking for new places to advertise their products. Recently, advertisers have tried putting ads on fruit, in public bathrooms, and even in graffiti—illegal writing on public buildings. Where will we see ads next?

AFTER READING

A. CHECK YOUR UNDERSTANDING Which sentences are true? Which sentences are false? Fill in (T) for *True* or (F) for *False*.

1. Advertising is getting people to buy products.	(T)	(F)
2. Product placement is an expensive way to advertise.	(T)	(F)
3. A product's image often influences people to buy it.	(T)	(F)
4. Advertisers don't use different types of advertising for different products.	(T)	(F)
5. Product placement means showing a commercial at a movie theater.	(T)	(F)

Reading Strategy

Finding Examples

Examples help you to understand the main ideas in a reading. Examples often follow the words *for example*, *for instance*, and *here are some examples*.

B. PRACTICE: FINDING EXAMPLES Look back at the reading on pages 94-95 and find the examples from the box. Underline them. Then match these examples with the ideas below.

a. Elliot and ET eat Reese's Pieces in *ET*.
b. Advertisers might create an image of luxury for a certain type of car.
c. Advertisers will suggest that a person who uses a certain shampoo will be popular.

Ideas

_______ **1.** Advertisers appeal to people's emotional needs.

_______ **2.** A product image is a value that the consumer connects with a product.

_______ **3.** With product placement, a product appears in a TV show, a movie, a music video, a book, or a computer game.

C. VOCABULARY CHECK Fill in the blanks with words and phrases from the box.

fact of life	name brands	qualities
~~image~~	personalize	

1. In an online commercial for a new computer, the hero is a scientist. The ______image______ for this product is intelligence.
2. When you go to a company website, you give information about yourself. Companies use this information to ____________ messages for you.
3. It won't be difficult to create a commercial for this product. It has many excellent ____________.
4. People often buy a product for its image. It's a ____________.
5. I don't recognize these types of shampoo. They're not ____________.

Reading Strategy

Recognizing Word Forms

Good readers recognize different forms of words. Endings on words sometimes show the part of speech. Here are some examples.

Ending	Part of Speech	Example
-ment	noun (for a thing)	improve**ment**
-er	noun (for a person)	help**er**
-ous	adjective	seri**ous**

 **D. PRACTICE: RECOGNIZING WORD FORMS** Look back at the reading on pages 94–95. Find forms of these words. Complete the chart.

Verb	Noun (thing)	Noun (person)	Adjective
advertise	advertisement	advertiser	
consume			
	fame		
	luxury		
place			
write			

E. MAKING CONNECTIONS: PARTS 2 AND 3 In small groups, discuss the BMW online commercial you read about on page 89. Why was it successful? What emotional need did it target? What product image did the advertisers create?

F. JOURNAL WRITING Choose *one* of these topics:

- advertisements at games or movies
- advertisements in the movies (product placement)
- buying something just for its image
- the worst ad or TV commercial
- your favorite ad or TV commercial

Write about this topic for five minutes. Don't worry about grammar. Don't use a dictionary.

PART 4 THE MECHANICS OF WRITING

In Part 5, you will describe a television commercial. You will need to use the simple present tense and make sure that subjects and verbs agree. You might also need to use the present continuous tense. You'll need adjectives and adverbs for your description. You'll also need words to show order in a story and the expressions *there is/are* and *it is.* Part 4 will help you learn how to use these.

The Present Continuous Tense

Use the present continuous tense to describe something that is happening now. Sometimes it can begin a description of a setting in a story or a scene in a commercial.

Examples: The hero **is driving** a sports car.
be + verb + ing

Two women **are walking** on the beach.
be + verb + ing

A. PRACTICE: SPELLING Use the spelling rules on page 168. Write the *–ing* form of each verb.

1. share sharing
2. do ______
3. solve ______
4. admire ______
5. advertise ______
6. make ______
7. study ______
8. sell ______

B. PRACTICE: THE PRESENT CONTINUOUS TENSE Fill in the blanks with the present continuous forms of the verbs in parentheses.

1. A man and a woman are driving (drive) an SUV on a dark road.
2. At the beginning of the shampoo commercial, a woman ______ (admire) her friend's hair.
3. The children ______ (talk), and they ______ (smile).
4. The women in this ad ______ (wear) expensive clothing.
5. A driver in this commercial ______ (sit) in his car.
   He ______ (study) a map.

Review: The Simple Present Tense

You can use the simple present to describe the events in a story or a scene in a commercial.

Examples: In the BMW commercial, the car **goes** around a curve, and a bear **appears**.

Subject-Verb Agreement

The subject of a sentence must agree with the verb. The subject and verb must agree in person (first, second, third) and in number (singular or plural).

Examples:

Third person singular: **He drives** an SUV. (simple present)
He is driving an SUV. (present continuous)

Third person plural: **They drive** a BMW. (simple present)
They are driving a BMW. (present continuous)

Note: *Couple* takes the singular form of the verb.

Example: The **couple drives** a Lexus.

Other words that take the singular form are *family, class*, and *group*.

C. PRACTICE: SUBJECT-VERB AGREEMENT Fill in the blanks with the correct forms of the verbs in parentheses.

Rob and Stacy ____are____ (be) driving to the beach. The couple ____________ (be) talking and laughing. Stacy ____________ (see) a dog in the road. She ____________ (say), "Look at that dog!" Rob ____________ (turn) and ____________ (notice) the dog. The dog ____________ (seem) lost. They ____________ (open) the car door, and the dog ________________ (jump) in the car.

Showing Order

You can give each event in a story a number or set it apart with a word such as *then*. This shows order. Begin the sentence with the number or order word. Put a comma after it.*

Examples: He's sitting at his desk. **First,** he makes a phone call. **Then** he writes an email. **After that**, he goes to the window. **Finally,** he leaves the room.

Words that show order include:

First,	At first,	At the beginning,
Then	Next,	After that,
After a while,	Finally,	At the end,

***Note:** Don't use a comma after *then*.

D. PRACTICE: SHOWING ORDER On a separate piece of paper, use the sentences below to write a paragraph. Use the events in the list. Use words that show order, such as *first* and *then*. Begin each order word with a capital letter. Use a comma if necessary.

First sentence: In this commercial, a mother and her son are playing in the park.

Event 1: The boy starts running.

Event 2: He falls down and hurts his knee.

Event 3: He starts crying.

Event 4: He runs to his mother.

Event 5: She puts a Spider-Man Band-Aid on his knee.

Event 6: The boy smiles.

Adjectives

Use adjectives with nouns to make your descriptions of people and things clear. Adjectives come before nouns or after the verb *be*.

Examples: He's driving a **new** BMW.
The BMW is **black**.

Adjectives also come after the verbs *seem* and *look*.

Examples: He **looks** nervous.
They **seem** happy.

E. PRACTICE: ADJECTIVES Think about five TV commercials you know. On a separate piece of paper, write five sentences about the commercials. Use adjectives in your sentences.

Example: The new milk commercial is **funny**.

Adverbs

Adverbs describe verbs. They answer the question *How.* You can form most adverbs from adjectives by adding the ending *–ly*.

Examples: A river moves **smoothly** to the ocean. (smooth ➜ smoothly)
My neighbor speaks very **quickly**. (quick ➜ quickly)

Some adverbs appear at the beginning of a sentence. When they appear at the beginning, put a comma after them.

Examples: **Suddenly,** it starts to rain.
Unexpectedly, the dog jumps into the car.

F. PRACTICE: ADVERBS Fill in the blanks with the adverb forms of the words in parentheses.

1. Jennifer learned to speak Japanese ______perfectly______ (perfect).

2. The little girl ____________________ (quiet) asked for some milk.

3. The professor wrote ____________________ (neat) on the board.

4. The dog ____________________ (quick) jumped into the truck.

5. The boy behaved very ____________________ (different) from the other children.

Words in Phrases: *It Is, There Is/Are*

We use *it is* and *there is/are* to describe a situation or a scene. Use *it is* to describe the weather, the temperature, or other conditions.

Examples: **It's** raining. **It's** cold.

Use *there is/are* to describe people or objects in a scene.

Examples: **There's** a dog in the back of the truck.
There are two children at the table.

Note: Use *there is* with a singular subject. Use *there are* with a plural subject.

G. PRACTICE: WORDS IN PHRASES In small groups, discuss one of the ads on page 92. Use *It is* and *There is/are.*

Example: **It's** dark. **There are** two people in a car.

H. REVIEW: EDITING A PARAGRAPH There are seven mistakes in this paragraph. They are mistakes with subject-verb agreement, verb tense, adverbs, and commas with adverbs and with order words. Find and correct them.

In this commercial, you see a small puppy. At the beginning, he ^is lying on the kitchen floor. He seem tired. There's a big bowl of food near him, but he doesn't eat it. He looks sad. Then, a woman comes into the kitchen. She calls the puppy, but he doesn't come. He just lie there. Next, she gives him a new kind of puppy food. The puppy try the food. He eats it loud. Suddenly the dog has energy. He look happy and alive. He runs across the room and jumps into the woman's arms.

PART 5 ACADEMIC WRITING

WRITING ASSIGNMENT

In Part 5, you will write one paragraph about a TV commercial.

MODEL

Here is a model of one student's work. First, just read the model. Don't write anything yet. You will follow these same steps beginning on page 106.

STEP A. CHOOSING A TOPIC Check (✓) a type of television commercial. Write your choice.

- ☐ an ad for shoes ____________________
- ☑ a car ad the ad for the new Lexus SUV
- ☐ a soft drink ad ____________________
- ☐ an ad for shampoo ____________________
- ☐ an ad for another product ____________________

STEP B. GETTING IDEAS Answer these questions. Write only short notes.

1. What product is the commercial advertising? What adjective describes this commercial?
Lexus SUV; exciting

2. What is happening at the beginning of the commercial? Describe the people or things that you see.
wealthy couple on dark road; happy and relaxed

3. What happens next? Describe the people or things that you see.
starts to rain; couple nervous

4. Then what happens? Describe the people or things that you see.
drive around curve—wild animals!

5. What happens after that? Describe the people or things that you see.
car stops quickly

6. What other events are there? Describe the people or things that you see.
animals and people look at each other

7. What happens in the end? Describe the people or things that you see.
animals quietly cross road; couple relaxed again and drives on

STEP C. WRITING COMPLETE SENTENCE Use your answers from Step B. Write them in complete sentences. Don't worry about spelling and grammar mistakes. (**Note:** There are some mistakes in the model sentences below.)

1. The television commercial for the new Lexus sport utility vehicle is exciting.
2. You see a wealthy couple in their Lexus SUV. They driving on a dark country road at night. They look happy and relaxed.
3. It starts to rain, and it get darker. The couple seems nervous.
4. They drive careful around a curve. There is two wild animals in the middle of the road.
5. The man stop the car immediately. It's raining, but the car stops quick and smoothly.
6. The animals looks at the couple; the couple looks at the animals.
7. The animals quietly cross the road. The man and woman looks relaxed again and they drive on safely.

STEP D. WRITING YOUR PARAGRAPH On a separate piece of paper, copy your sentences from Step C. You can combine two sentences if you want to. Use paragraph form. Indent the first line. After each period, continue on the same line. Don't worry about mistakes.

The television commercial for the new Lexus sport utility vehicle is exciting. First you see a wealthy couple in their Lexus SUV. They driving on a dark country road at night. They look happy and relaxed. Then, it starts to rain, and it get darker. Now the couple seems nervous. They drive careful around a curve. Suddenly, there is two wild animals in the middle of the road. The man stop the car immediately. It's raining, but the car stops quick and smoothly. The animals looks at the couple; the couple looks at the animals. Finally, the animals quietly cross the road. The man and woman looks relaxed again and they drive on safely.

STEP E. EDITING Read your paragraph and look for mistakes with:

- tenses (present and present continuous)
- subject-verb agreement
- punctuation with *first, then, after that, now, finally*
- adjectives
- adverbs
- *it is; there is/are*

STEP F. REWRITING Write your paragraph again, without the mistakes.

The television commercial for the new Lexus sport utility vehicle is exciting. First, you see a wealthy couple in their Lexus SUV. They're driving on a dark country road at night. They look happy and relaxed. Then it starts to rain, and it gets darker. Now, the couple seems nervous. They drive carefully around a curve. Suddenly, there are two wild animals in the middle of the road. The man stops the car immediately. It's raining, but the car stops quickly and smoothly. The animals look at the couple. The couple looks at the animals. Finally, the animals quietly cross the road. The man and woman look relaxed again, and they drive on safely.

YOUR TURN

Now follow Steps A-F to write your own paragraph about a TV commercial.

STEP A. CHOOSING A TOPIC Check (✓) a type of television commercial. Write your choice.

- ☐ an ad for shoes ______________________
- ☐ a car ad ______________________
- ☐ a soft drink ad ______________________
- ☐ an ad for shampoo ______________________
- ☐ an ad for another product ______________________

STEP B. GETTING IDEAS Answer these questions. Write only short notes.

1. What product is the commercial advertising? What adjective describes this commercial?

____

2. What is happening at the beginning of the commercial? Describe the people or things that you see.

____

3. What happens next? Describe the people or things that you see. ______________________

____

4. Then what happens? Describe the people or things that you see. ______________________

____

5. What happens after that? Describe the people or things that you see. ______________________

____

6. What other events are there? Describe the people or things that you see. ______________________

____

7. What happens in the end? Describe the people or things that you see. ______________________

____

STEP C. WRITING COMPLETE SENTENCES Use your answers from Step B. Write them in complete sentences. Don't worry about spelling and grammar mistakes.

1. ____

____

2. ____

____

3. ____________________

____

4. ____________________

____

5. ____________________

____

6. ____________________

____

7. ____________________

____

Writing Strategy

Writing a Paragraph

A paragraph has one topic sentence. One sentence in the paragraph expresses the main idea. It's usually the first sentence. The rest of the sentences give more information about the main idea. These sentences often connect to each other with words such as *first, then,* and *finally*.

Remember: Indent the first line in a paragraph. End each sentence with a period. After each period, continue on the same line.

STEP D. WRITING YOUR PARAGRAPH On a separate piece of paper, copy your sentences from Step C. You can combine two sentences if you want to. Use paragraph form. Indent the first line. After each period, continue on the same line. Don't worry about mistakes.

STEP E. EDITING Read your paragraph and look for mistakes with:

- tenses (present and present continuous)
- subject-verb agreement
- punctuation with *first, then, after that, now, finally*
- adjectives
- adverbs
- *it is; there is/are*

STEP F. REWRITING Write your paragraph again, without the mistakes.

UNIT 2 VOCABULARY WORKSHOP

Review vocabulary items you learned in Chapters 3 and 4.

A. MATCHING Match the definitions with the words. Write the correct letters on the lines.

Words	Definitions
______ **1.** attract	~~**a.**~~ a group of people who want to buy something
______ **2.** effective	**b.** show
______ **3.** ancient	**c.** It's too bad, but…
______ **4.** reflect	**d.** people who admire sports teams and players
__a__ **5.** market	**e.** look good to someone
______ **6.** unfortunately	**f.** get better
______ **7.** fans	**g.** male or female
______ **8.** improve	**h.** from very old times
______ **9.** income	**i.** successful
______ **10.** gender	**j.** money that people make from work

B. SENTENCE HALVES Match the first half of the sentences with the correct second half. Write the correct letters on the lines.

__d__ **1.** **Name brand products** are…	**a.** attract consumers to their products.
______ **2.** We can **acquire** understanding…	**b.** in chess.
______ **3.** By **clicking a button**,…	**c.** ancient people.
______ **4.** **Advertisers** hope to…	~~**d.**~~ usually expensive.
______ **5.** She's an **expert**…	**e.** from experts.
______ **6.** An **archaeologist** studies…	**f.** you can buy almost anything on the Internet.

C. WORDS IN PHRASES: PREPOSITIONS Which prepositions can you put together with the words in blue? Fill in the blanks with words from the box. Use two of these prepositions more than once.

about	in	of	to

1. Jason wants a **career** ______in______ computer programming.
2. He's **crazy** ____________ computers.
3. He plans to **major** ____________ computer science.
4. He learned about the program at Valley College from **word** ____________ **mouth**.
5. Jason and three of his friends **belong** ____________ the Computer Club.
6. He's **aware** ____________ one problem: many people are studying this subject these days, so it might be difficult to find a job in the future.
7. However, he believes that computers are **here** ____________ **stay**.
8. He thinks there will be jobs for anyone who wants to **work** ____________ computer programming.

D. WHICH WORD DOESN'T BELONG? In each row, cross out the word without a connection to the other words.

1. stress	emphasize	~~admire~~
2. commercials	highlights	advertisements
3. strength	career	profession
4. counselor	talent	mentor
5. psychology	archaeology	discovery
6. image	suggestions	advice
7. consumers	fans	logos
8. effective	irritating	useful

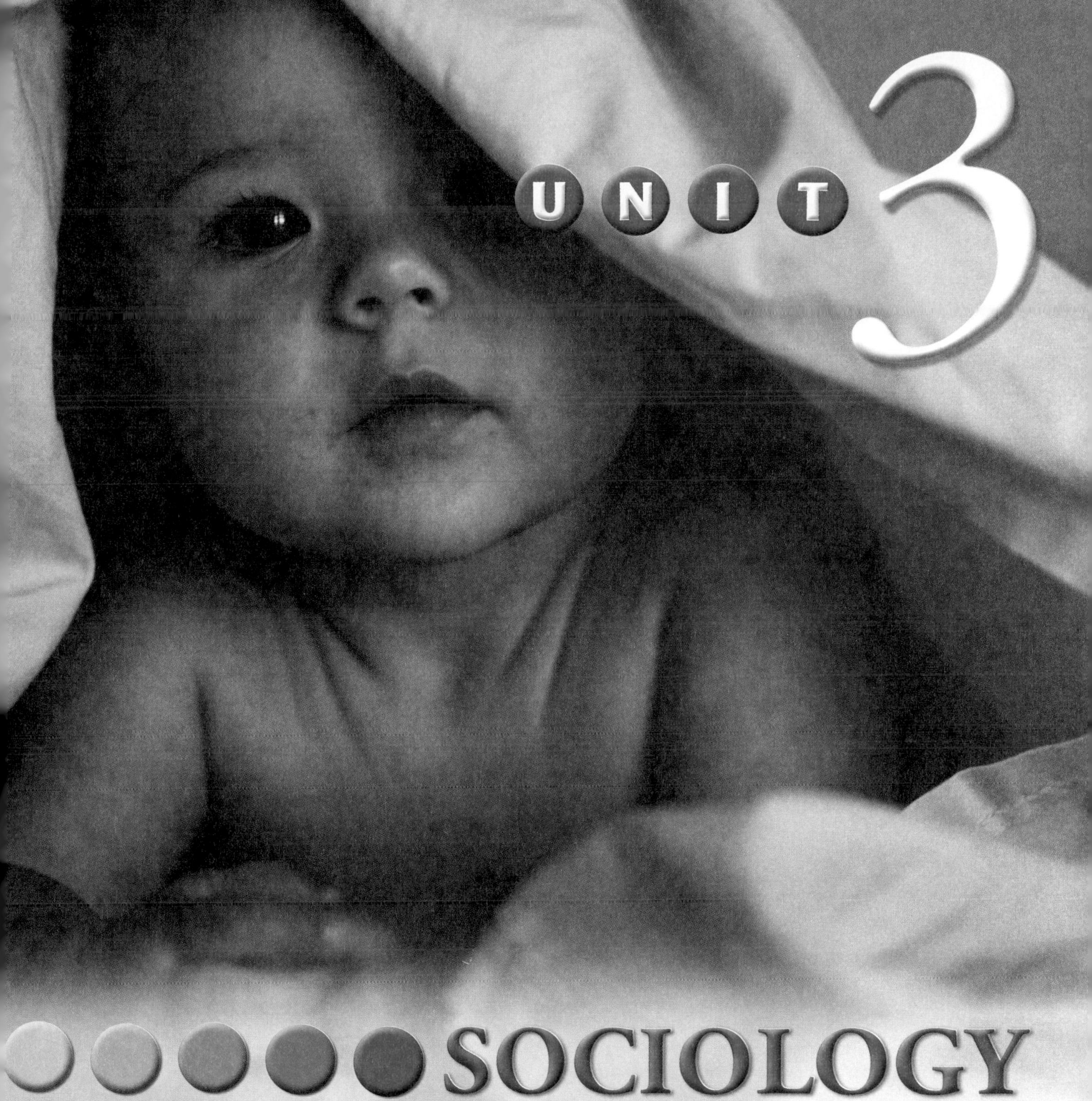

SOCIOLOGY

Chapter 5
Parenting, Gender, and Stereotypes

Chapter 6
Becoming a Member of a Community

CHAPTER 5

Parenting, Gender, and Stereotypes

Discuss the questions.

- Look at the picture. What are the man and boy doing?
- What are three things your parents taught you to do as a child?
- Do you think parents should treat their sons and daughters the same? Explain your answer.
- Read the chapter title. What do you think the chapter will be about?

PART 1 INTRODUCTION Parenting in Chimp Society

BEFORE READING

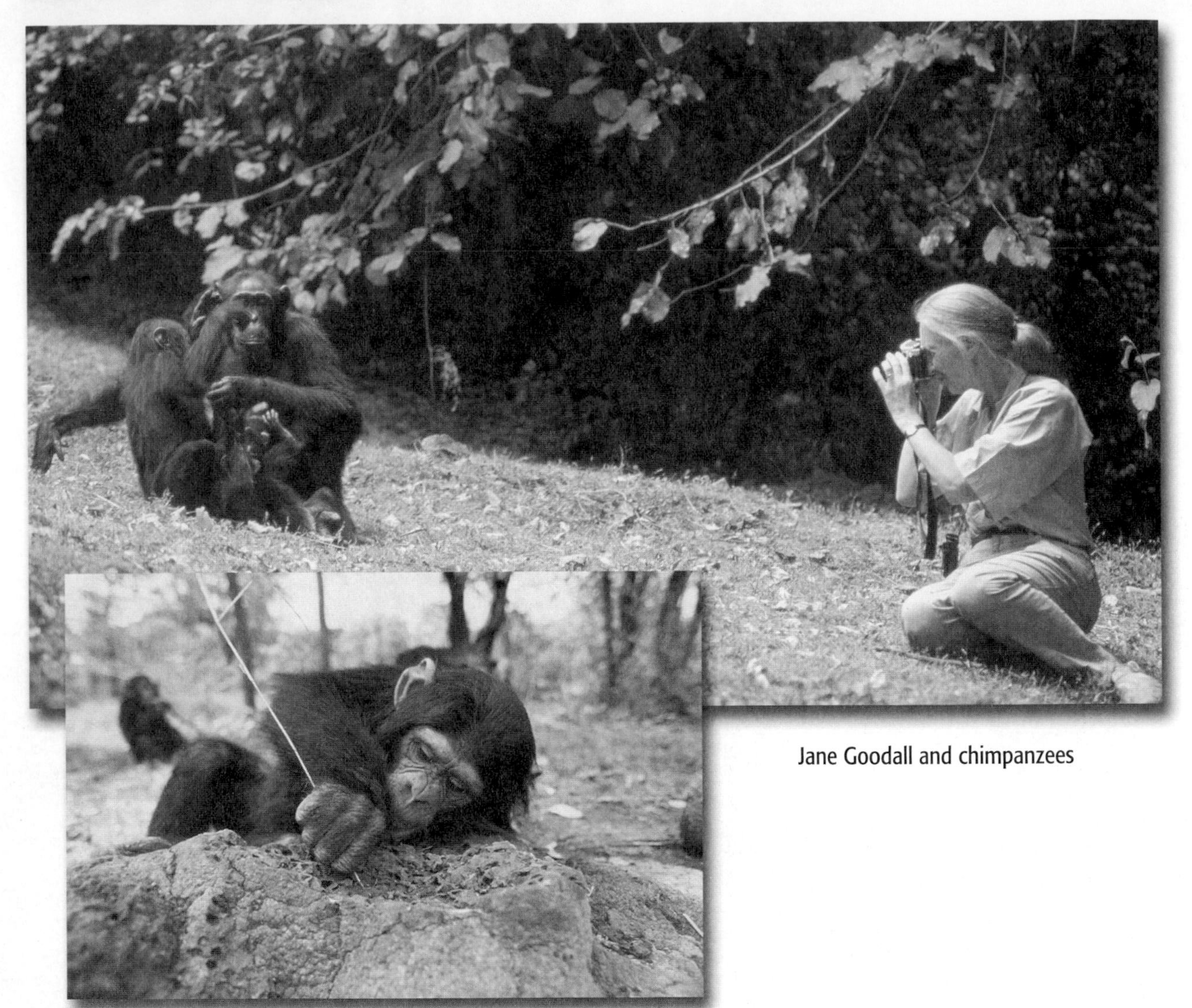

Jane Goodall and chimpanzees

What is the chimpanzee doing?

THINKING AHEAD Look at the pictures. Answer these questions with a partner.

1. What might be happening in these pictures?
2. Can chimps use tools? Explain your answer.
3. How might chimpanzees (chimps) be similar to humans?
4. Do chimps learn from each other? Explain your answer.

READING

Read about Jane Goodall and her study of chimps. As you read, think about this question:

• How is the society of chimpanzees similar to human society?

Parenting in Chimp Society

Jane Goodall always had a passion for animals—horses, dogs, birds, and everything else. She grew up in England but dreamed of Africa. Her dream came true in 1960. Her employer and mentor, the famous Louis Leakey, sent her to Tanganyika (now Tanzania) to study chimpanzees. She was 26 years old, and she expected to stay there for a few months. However, the study of the chimps in Tanganyika became her life's work. She was the first person to seriously study chimps in the wild—in nature, not in zoos. Jane Goodall's discoveries changed everything for primatologists—scientists who study animals such as gorillas and chimps.

Introduction to the Chimps of Gombe

Goodall lived in the wild area of Gombe—many miles from any town. There were dangers all around, from sickness (especially malaria) and animals such as deadly snakes and leopards. Goodall was afraid, but not of sickness or wild animals. She was afraid it might be impossible to get close to the chimps and to learn their secrets. At first, they were afraid of *her* and ran away when they saw her. Every day, she took a little food, a notebook, and some binoculars and walked to a high place in the forest. She sat for hours and hours. She heard the chimps far away and sometimes saw them with her binoculars. Slowly, they became less shy, less afraid of the "strange white chimp." However, it took almost a year before they allowed her to come close.

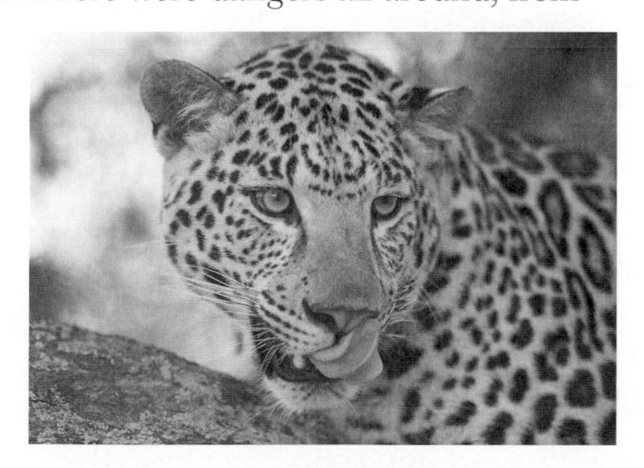

A leopard

Binoculars

Chimps: Social Primates

Goodall learned that in many ways, chimp society is similar to human society. Maybe this isn't surprising because almost 99 percent of chimp DNA is the same as human DNA. Like humans, chimps live in groups. Each member has a position in the group, and there is one male leader. Like humans, most chimps have especially close connections to their mothers and their siblings—their brothers and sisters. Also similar to humans, some female chimps are better mothers than others. One chimp at Gombe (Goodall called her "Flo") was a wonderful mother. Flo was loving toward her infants. She played with her babies, carried them on her back, and kept them from danger.

60 During Goodall's time at Gombe, she married and had her own baby. She said she learned how to be a mother from three teachers: "There was my own mother, there was Dr. Spock [an 65 expert in child psychology]—and there was Flo."

Learning

Chimps are similar to humans in 70 another way. They *learn* through life. They learn by playing with 75 things in the forest, like human children play with toys.

Flo and her baby

They also learn by watching their 80 mothers and siblings. One of Goodall's most important discoveries was the chimps' ability to use tools. In the past, primatologists believed that only humans used tools. They were wrong. 85 Chimps at Gombe use a thin piece of a tree, a twig, as a tool. They use this twig to get termites (a type of insect) to eat. They do not do this naturally. Both males and females have to *learn* how to 90 use twigs from their mothers. However, there is a gender difference. Young females learn faster because they spend more time with their mothers, more time in "twig-using lessons." Young 95 males spend more time with other young males, and they learn to hunt for meat, a necessary source of protein. However, the males don't often share meat with the females, so termites are 100 an important food for females.

AFTER READING

A. CHECK YOUR UNDERSTANDING Which sentences are true? Which sentences are false? Fill in (T) for *True* or (F) for *False*.

1. In the beginning, the chimps were afraid of Jane Goodall. (T) (F)
2. There are many similarities between chimp and human societies. (T) (F)
3. Goodall learned how to be a good mother, in part, from a chimp. (T) (F)
4. Only humans use tools. (T) (F)
5. Unlike humans, chimps do everything naturally. They don't learn from other chimps. (T) (F)

B. TALK ABOUT IT Answer these questions in small groups.

1. According to the reading, what are some similarities between chimps and humans? How many similarities can you find in the reading?
2. You read that chimps "learn by playing with things in the forest, like human children play with toys." What might be some "toys" for chimps? What might chimps "learn" from these "toys"?

PART 2 GENERAL INTEREST READING
Children, Gender, and Toys

BEFORE READING

A. THINKING AHEAD Read the questions below and think about them for a minute. Ask classmates for their opinions. Record their answers on the questionnaire (𝍸 = 5 people answered this, for example).

Questionnaire

Who is better at these subjects in school?	**Boys**	**Girls**	**Both**	**Neither**
• math				
• language				
• physical education				
• reading				
Who usually enjoys these activities?	**Boys**	**Girls**	**Both**	**Neither**
• playing a game with a group of children				
• talking with a "best friend"				
Who enjoys playing with these toys?	**Boys**	**Girls**	**Both**	**Neither**
• a toy house				
• a toy airplane				

B. VOCABULARY PREPARATION Read the sentences below. The words in blue are from the next reading. Match the definitions in the box with the words in blue. Write the correct letters on the lines.

> **a.** ability to take one of many possible things
> **b.** female child
> **c.** get ready
> **~~d.~~** male child
> **e.** babies
> **f.** scientists who study society and humans in groups
> **g.** separate something into its pieces
> **h.** the time of life when a person is an adult

______ **1.** Psychologists, **sociologists**, and experts in education are looking for the answers to two important questions.

______ **2.** At birth, female **infants** make more sounds than newborn male babies.

______ **3.** The Hongs have two boys, but they're hoping to have a **daughter** next year.

__d__ **4.** The Garcias have three girls, but they're hoping to have a **son** in a year or two.

______ **5.** We need to **take apart** this cellphone and find out what's wrong with it.

______ **6.** I have to **prepare** for a big exam in my sociology class.

______ **7.** Children's activities and games are one kind of preparation for **adulthood**.

______ **8.** The children have a **choice** of any toy in the room. They can take any toy that they want.

Reading Strategy

Guessing the Meanings of New Words: *In Other Words*

You don't always need a dictionary to guess the meaning of a new word. Sometimes a definition or explanation of the word comes after the phrase *in other words.*

Example: Female infants are more **mature** than male infants. **In other words,** (they seem a little older) than baby boys.

C. GUESSING THE MEANINGS OF NEW WORDS: *IN OTHER WORDS* As you read, look for meanings of new words after the phrase *in other words.*

READING

Read about the importance of toys. As you read, think about these questions:

- Why are toys important?
- What advice about toys do educators and sociologists have for parents?

Children, Gender, and Toys

Watch a group of children in a classroom or at play. You will probably notice many differences. The children have different abilities, interests, and personalities. However, in several important ways, the boys seem similar to each other, and the girls seem similar to each other. In many cultures, boys are usually better at math and physical education. Girls are generally better at reading and language. Boys enjoy *doing* things such as playing games with a group of boys. Girls enjoy *talking* with a "best friend." Surprisingly, this can be true even of a set of twins that is a boy and a girl. These twins share many of the same genes, have the same parents, and grow up in the same environment. But they often have very different abilities and interests. Psychologists, sociologists, and experts in education are looking for the answers to two questions: What are the reasons for these gender differences—nature or nurture? And how do children's activities influence their adult lives?

The Influence of Nature

Gender differences begin with nature, but nurture plays an important role, too. At birth, female infants are naturally a little more mature than male infants. In other words, newborn baby girls seem a little older, more "adult" than baby boys. They have the ability for longer eye contact; they can look into their parents' eyes without looking away. Also, newborn baby girls are more vocal; in other words, they make more noises or sounds than male infants make. They seem to "talk" to their parents. This is *nature*. Their parents respond by talking to them. This is *nurture*. It might surprise many parents to learn this, but they talk more to their daughters than to their sons. Girls' abilities in reading and language might begin with the babies' nature, but the parents' response is nurture.

The Influence of Toys

Toys also influence the amount of conversation—in other words, how much talking there is—and the amount of activity. A study by the University of California at Santa Cruz focused on the choice of children's toys. Psychologists gave two different toys to both male and female children. One was a toy car. The children could take it apart and put the pieces back together. Most people think of this as a toy for boys. The other toy was a grocery store—in other words, a toy supermarket with food and other products. Most people think of this as a "girl's toy." The researchers' discovery was interesting but maybe not surprising: the toy grocery store involved much more *conversation* than the toy car. Girls usually play with toys such as grocery stores, so they practice more language than boys do. Boys usually play with toys like cars, so they practice *doing* things such as problem solving. However, they don't practice much language.

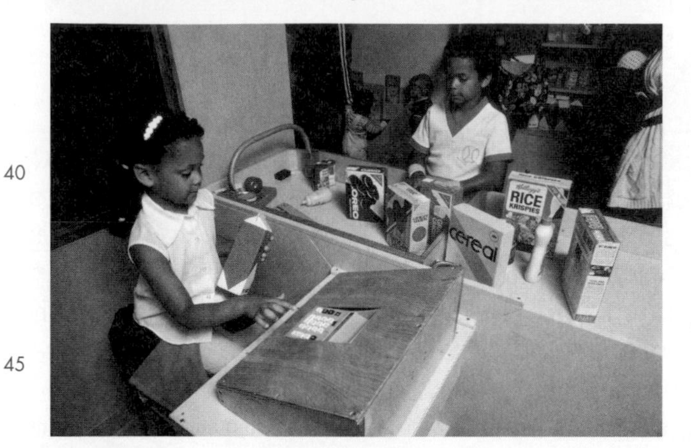

Toys also determine the *type* of conversation, according to another study at the University of California. Typical girls' toys, such as the grocery store, involve social conversation. This type of conversation is important in relationships—in other words, with family and personal connections. Typical boys' toys, like the take-apart car, involve the language of tasks—in other words, giving and following instructions. This type of conversation is important for adults who have careers.

According to educators and sociologists, playing with toys prepares children for adult life. With toys, children practice language and activities that are necessary in adulthood. The type of toy determines the type of practice and preparation. Most parents never think about this. They give typical girls' toys to a daughter, so she prepares for relationships, but she doesn't prepare for a career. They give typical boys' toys to a son, so he prepares for the world of work, but he doesn't prepare for personal relationships. Most parents aren't aware of this possible problem.

The Influence of Parents

Parents can't change nature, but they can influence their children's choice of toys. In a toy store, the cars attract the boys, and the grocery stores appeal to the girls. This seems to be nature, and nothing can change it. However, parents can encourage their children to play with *both* types of toys. They can sometimes buy a "girl's toy" for a son to help him prepare for future relationships. They can sometimes buy a "boy's toy" for a daughter to help her prepare for a future career. These might not be the child's favorite toys, but they are an important influence on the child's adult life. As some people say, "Play is the work of children."

AFTER READING

A. CHECK YOUR UNDERSTANDING Which statements about how children develop are true? Look at this list and check (✓) the correct answers.

_______ **1.** Both nature and nurture determine gender differences.

_______ **2.** Parents talk more to their sons than to their daughters.

_______ **3.** The type of toy determines how much language children practice.

_______ **4.** Typical girls' toys involve the practice of social conversation.

_______ **5.** Typical toys for boys involve the practice of conversation that people use in work situations.

_______ **6.** Parents should not give typical girls' toys to their sons.

B. FINDING DETAILS You learned in Chapter 2 that graphic organizers, like the tree diagram below, can help you visualize the main ideas and details in a reading. Fill in the tree diagram below to answer this question: What is the influence of toys on a child?

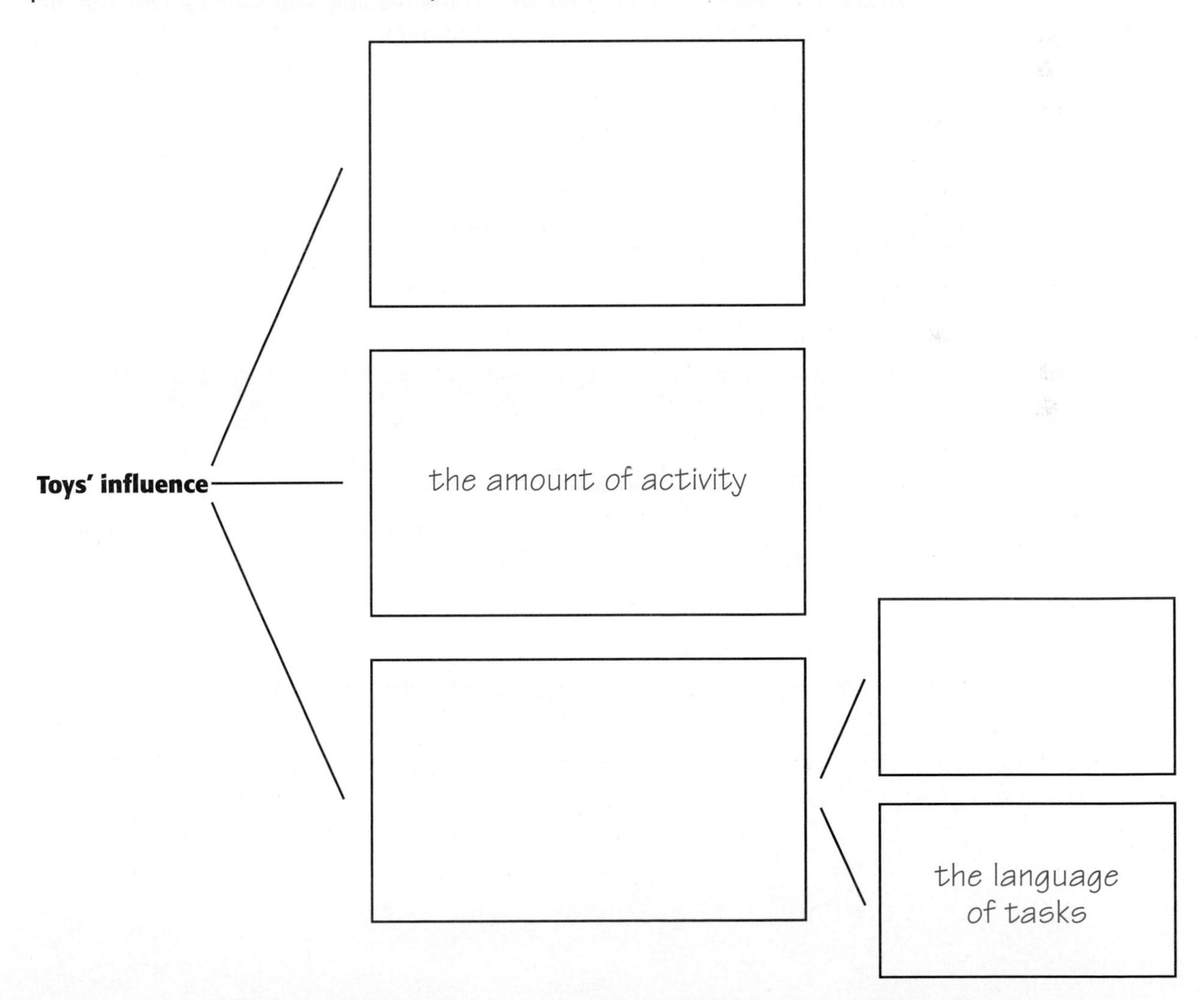

C. VOCABULARY CHECK Fill in the blanks with words and phrases from the box.

amount	grocery store	tasks
~~eye contact~~	relationships	vocal

1. In some cultures, ___eye contact___ is important, but in other cultures, people *don't* look into other people's eyes very much.
2. My family is very ______________. They talk and sing a lot.
3. We need some milk, so I'm going to the ______________ to get some.
4. Toys influence the ______________ of conversation—how much talking there is.
5. These ______________ are part of doing this job.
6. My ______________ with friends and family members are important to me.

D. VOCABULARY EXTENSION: WORDS WITH *–HOOD* In the reading, you saw the word *adulthood.* It means "the state of being an adult." Below are definitions for other words with *–hood*. Write the correct words on the lines.

1. the state of being a child: ___childhood___
2. the state of being a parent: ______________
3. the state of being a mother: ______________
4. the state of being a father: ______________

Reading Strategy

Infinitives of Purpose

An infinitive (*to* + the simple form of a verb) can give the purpose of an action—in other words, the reason for the action. An infinitive can answer *Why.*

Examples: Louis Leakey sent Jane Goodall to Tanzania **to study** chimpanzees.
Chimps in Gombe use a twig **to get** termites.

E. PRACTICE: INFINITIVES OF PURPOSE Look back at the reading on pages 119–120. Find infinitives to answer these questions. (The line numbers where the infinitives can be found are in parentheses.)

1. Why might parents sometimes buy a "girl's toy" for their son? (68)
2. Why might parents sometimes buy a "boy's toy" for their daughter? (69)

Reading Strategy

Understanding the Word *So*

The word *so* has several meanings. One common meaning is "that's why." *So* comes after an explanation of reason or purpose.

Example: Male chimps don't often share meat with the females, **so** termites are an important food for females.

F. PRACTICE: UNDERSTANDING THE WORD *SO* Look back at the reading on pages 119–120 for the word *so*. Answer these questions. Hint: The answers are in lines 32–50.

1. Why do girls practice more language than boys do?
2. Why do boys practice doing things such as problem solving?

G. APPLICATION Discuss the questions below in small groups.

1. What toys did you play with when you were young?
2. What did you learn from those toys?

PART 3 ACADEMIC READING Stereotypes and Their Effects

BEFORE READING

Reading Strategy

Previewing a Reading

It's a good idea to look quickly at a reading passage (an article or chapter, for example) before reading it. This helps you think of questions before you read, and you can understand more. One way to preview a reading is to look at the headings—the titles for each section. In the reading starting on page 126, the first reading is "Gender Stereotypes." It appears after Line 15.

A. PRACTICE: PREVIEWING A READING Look at the headings on pages 126–127. Then answer these questions with a partner.

1. What words in the headings do you know?
2. What might this reading be about?
3. Think of one question that the reading might answer.

B. VOCABULARY PREPARATION Read the sentences on the next page. The words in blue are from the next reading. Match the definitions in the box with the words in blue. Write the correct letters on the lines.

a. groups of humans who share similar physical characteristics
b. have a picture in mind
c. "more bad"
d. old
e. people who study a subject to learn something new
f. what people learn from doing research
g. not specific; without details

b 1. **Imagine** a group of students in a college classroom. Can you visualize them?

_____ 2. Dylan had a problem with his paragraph. It was too **general**, so he needed to add some specific information.

_____ 3. Melissa has several different **races** in her family: her mother is white, her father is Asian, and her uncle is black.

_____ 4. I'm really interested in that study. What did the **researchers** learn from it?

_____ 5. The **results** of the study were surprising. The scientists were surprised by the answers they found.

_____ 6. My sister plays tennis better than I do. However, my brother plays **worse** than I do, so I don't feel so bad about it.

_____ 7. Everyone in the group was **elderly**. Some were over the age of 65, but most were over 70.

Reading Strategy

Guessing the Meanings of New Words: *That Is*

When you come to a new word in a reading, you don't always need a dictionary. Sometimes there is a definition or an explanation after the phrase *that is*. *That is* might define or explain one word, another phrase, or an idea. *That is* means the same as *in other words*. There is a comma after *that is*.

Example: They **briefly** discussed the chapter. **That is**, they talked (for only a short time.)

C. GUESSING THE MEANINGS OF NEW WORDS: *THAT IS* As you read, look for meanings of new words after the phrase *that is*.

READING

Read about stereotypes and how they affect people. As you read, think about these questions:

- What are stereotypes?
- How do they influence people?

Stereotypes and Their Effects

Imagine a specific group of people. Let's call them "Xenrovians." People have beliefs about a typical Xenrovian. They say, "He's Xenrovian, so he probably belongs to the upper class, thinks that expensive name-brand products are important, and is not very mentally aware. But he's really good at golf." Most people with these beliefs do not *know* any Xenrovians, or maybe they met a Xenrovian once. Their beliefs are stereotypes—generalized ideas about a group of people. Some stereotypes are positive (for example, "good at golf"), and some are negative (for example, "not very mentally aware"), but all share one characteristic: they are too general, so they are usually *wrong*. There are stereotypes of races (white, black, etc.), ethnic groups (people of different cultures), ages (young, old), and both genders. Several universities are studying the effects of stereotypes on people during tests of ability. Psychologists and sociologists want to know the answer to this question: What is the influence of stereotypes on the *targets* of those stereotypes—for example, on Xenrovians? An article in *Newsweek* magazine gives the results of these studies.

Gender Stereotypes

In North America, there is a stereotype that women are not good at math. To test the effect of this stereotype, scientists at the University of Waterloo, in Canada, gave a math exam to a group of female and male students. All of the students were good at math, and math was important to them. Before the exam, researchers showed TV commercials to the students. One group of students—let's call them Group A—saw commercials with female stereotypes. Group B saw commercials without such stereotypes. The results were interesting. The women in Group A did worse than the men in Group A. They also did worse than the women in Group B. The researchers came to this conclusion: negative stereotypes of women influence the targets of the stereotypes (that is, women) in a negative way.

Ethnic Groups and Gender

The real purpose of a study at Harvard University was to see the effect of stereotypes. However, the 46 female Asian-American students thought it was only a difficult math exam. Before the test, the women had to fill out a questionnaire. For half of the women (let's call them Group A), the questions emphasized their ethnic group. One question, for example, was "When did your family first come to the United States?" For the other 50 percent, Group B, the questions emphasized their gender. In other words, the questionnaire reminded some women, "you are Asian," and others, "you are female." The results of the exam were very different for the two groups. Group A did much better than Group B. Group A got 54 percent right, but Group B got only 43 percent right. The reason? The questionnaire reminded Group A of a positive stereotype about their group: Asians do well at math. It reminded Group B of a negative stereotype in the United States: women don't do well at math.

Racial Stereotypes

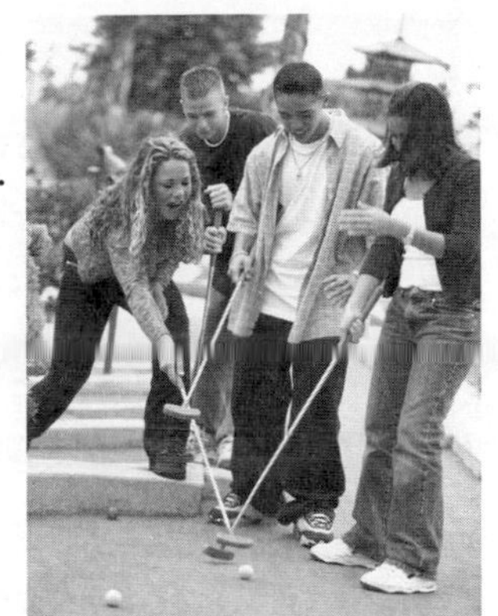

Researchers at Princeton University tested 40 black and 40 white male students to find the effect of racial stereotypes. The students did not know the real purpose of the study. (This is normal in psychological and scientific studies.) In the study, the students each played a game of mini golf. Before the game, researchers told some of the students (Group A), "This is a test of natural physical ability" in sports. Researchers told other students (Group B), "This is a test of mental strategies." Then the students (who did not usually play mini-golf) played the game. The results? In Group A, black students did better. In Group B, white students did better.

Stereotypes of Age

At Yale University, elderly people (all over age 60) took a test of memory. However, before the test, half of the people (Group A) briefly saw words such as "Alzheimer's"—that is, words with a negative meaning for elderly people. The other half (Group B) saw words such as "wise"—that is, positive words about elderly people. On the memory test, Group A did worse. Group B always did better, sometimes 64 percent better.

What Research Tells Us

Visualize, again, our Xenrovian. Imagine him in a classroom. He is going to take a test of mental ability. Just before the exam, someone reminds him of his ethnicity. She asks him, "What part of Xenrovia are you from?" The next day, he is outside. He is going to play a game of golf. Just before the game, another player asks him, "Did you learn to play golf in Xenrovia?" What effect are these questions going to have on him?

In these studies of people performing mental and physical tasks, all of the research came to the same conclusion: stereotypes of gender, race, ethnic group, and age have an effect on people. Specifically, they have an influence on the targets of stereotypes. A few people might not be aware of a stereotype of their group, so the stereotype doesn't influence them. However, most people are very aware. This news is mostly bad but possibly good. Negative stereotypes have a negative effect, so they can be dangerous, but positive stereotypes can have a positive effect. This is the encouraging news. One researcher has an interesting idea. To improve the results on a test, he thinks the professor needs to remind students, "You are Stanford students!" That is, the professor needs to remind them of a positive stereotype—that they go to a very good university. However, reminding students of their school's reputation would not be helpful at every university!

AFTER READING

Reading Strategy

Finding the Main Idea: Using Topic Sentences

Most paragraphs have a **topic sentence**. The topic sentence gives the main idea of the paragraph. In many paragraphs, the topic sentence is the first sentence.

A. PRACTICE: USING TOPIC SENTENCES Go back to the reading. Underline the first sentence of Paragraphs 2–5 (Lines 16–58).

B. FINDING THE MAIN IDEA In the reading, the first paragraph does not give the main idea. Instead, it asks a question. Underline the question in the first paragraph. The last paragraph is the conclusion. It answers the question. In the last paragraph, underline the two sentences that answer the question. This is the main idea.

C. VOCABULARY CHECK To answer these questions, look for *that is* in the lines in parentheses.

1. Who are the targets of stereotypes of women? (28) ______________________________

   ____

2. What is an example of a word with a negative meaning? (55) ______________________________

   ____

3. What is an example of a word with a positive meaning? (56) ______________________________

   ____

4. What is a stereotype of "Stanford students"? (74–75) ______________________________

   ____

D. REVIEW: INFINITIVES OF PURPOSE Fill in this chart with specific information from the reading. In the *Purpose of the Study* column, use an infinitive (*to* + simple form of a verb).

University	Tested	Purpose of the Study
University of Waterloo	math	to test the effects of a gender stereotype
Harvard		

Critical Thinking Strategy

Making Inferences

Sometimes a reading does not state something directly. Instead, the writer only suggests the meaning, and the reader needs to figure it out. This is an **inference**.

E. PRACTICE: MAKING INFERENCES Look back at the reading on pages 126–127. What inferences can you make? Line numbers are in parentheses.

1. According to the reading, what is a positive stereotype of black men? What is a positive stereotype of white men? (45–52)

 ____

 ____

2. Why did Group A of the Yale University Study do worse? Why did Group B do better? (53–58)

 ____

 ____

3. What effects will the question about golf have on the Xenrovian? (1–4; 59–63)

 ____

 ____

4. Why won't the professor's solution work for students at every university? (72–77)

 ____

 ____

F. MAKING CONNECTIONS Look back at the reading in Part 2 (pages 119–120). With a partner, answer these questions on a separate piece of paper.

1. Many children play only with toys typical of their gender. What is an example of a stereotypical female toy? What is an example of a stereotypical male toy?
2. What positive stereotype do girls learn about their gender from these toys?
3. What positive stereotype do boys learn about their gender from these toys?
4. What negative stereotype do girls learn about their gender from these toys?
5. What negative stereotype do boys learn about their gender from these toys?

G. JOURNAL WRITING Choose *one* of these topics:

- my favorite toy when I was a child
- something I learned about the importance of toys
- an effect of a stereotype on me

Write about this topic for five minutes. Don't worry about grammar. Don't use a dictionary.

PART 4 THE MECHANICS OF WRITING

In Part 5, you will write about a toy or activity from your childhood (the time when you were a child). You will need to use the word *when*, the word *so* or other conjunctions, the phrase *used to,* or other phrases with prepositions. Part 4 will help you learn how to use these.

Using the Word *When*

Use the word *when* to show the time that something happens, happened, or is going to happen. There are two ways to use it. When the word *when* is at the beginning of a sentence, add a comma. When it is in the middle of a sentence, do not add a comma.

Examples: **When** I was a child, we lived far from the city.

We lived far from the city **when** I was a child.

A. PRACTICE: USING THE WORD *WHEN* On a separate piece of paper, answer these questions. Use the word *when* in each sentence.

1. Where did you live when you were a child? When I was a child, I lived...
2. When you were a child, what were your favorite toys?
3. When you played with your friends, what were your favorite activities?
4. Did you create any games when you played with your friends?
5. Do you have happy memories when you think about your childhood?

Using the Word *So*

One meaning of *so* is *that's why*. When *so* means *that's why*, use a comma before *so*.

Example: The chimps were afraid of Goodall at first, **so** they stayed far away.

B. PRACTICE: USING THE WORD *SO* On a separate piece of paper, combine these sentences. Use the word *so* in each combination.

1. I was a girl. My parents gave me typical girls' toys. I was a girl, so my parents gave me typical girls' toys.
2. I had two brothers. There were a lot of toys for boys around the house.
3. We lived far from other houses. There weren't many other girls to play with.
4. There weren't a lot of children around. I played with my brothers.
5. I played with my brothers. I learned typical boys' games from them.

Review: Conjunctions

The words *and, but, or,* and *so* are **conjunctions**. They join (put together) ideas, words, or phrases.

Conjunction	Purpose	Examples
and	to join two or more similar ideas	I have a brother **and** a sister. We played with cars, toy houses, **and** balls.* I loved the movies**, and** I liked making little films at home with my father's video camera.
but	to join opposite things or ideas	There were always a lot of children and animals around our house **but** not many toys. I had a happy childhood**, but** we didn't have much money.
or	1. for possibilities 2. to join two negative ideas	We played with each other**, or** sometimes we just read wonderful adventure books. We played in all sorts of weather—rain, sun**, or** snow.* We didn't need a lot of money **or** toys.
so	to show the cause (reason) and the effect (result)	We didn't have a lot of toys**, so** we had to be creative and make our own games.

Punctuation: With these conjunctions, the general rule is the same. Use a comma before the conjunction when there is a subject and verb after it. When there isn't a subject and verb after the conjunction, do not use a comma before it.

***Exception:** With *and* and *or* use a comma before the last item in a list of things.

What is one difference between *so* and the other conjunctions? Look at the punctuation in the examples.

C. PRACTICE: CONJUNCTIONS On a separate piece of paper, combine these sentences. Use the word *and, but, or,* or *so* in each combination. If possible, combine the sentences in two ways—with and without a comma.

1. We ran. We jumped. We swam. We ran, jumped, and swam.
2. I played with my sister. I played with the kids in the neighborhood. (Do this two ways.)
3. We didn't watch much TV. We didn't go to the movies.
4. We had fun. We didn't have a lot of toys. (Do this two ways.)
5. We played outside. We played inside on rainy days. (Do this two ways.)
6. I played with both boys and girls. I practiced both social language and the language of tasks.
7. I was the writer. I was the director. I was the star of the movie.
8. I was happy. The other kids weren't.

Using the Phrase *Used To*

Use the phrase *used to* + the simple form of the verb for a past action that happened often in the past but doesn't happen now.

Example: When I was a child, we **used to go** to the beach every summer.

D. PRACTICE: USING THE PHRASE *USED TO* Read the questions in the chart and think about them for a minute. Ask five students the same questions. Record their answers on the chart.

Student	What toys did you use to play with when you were a child?	What used to be your favorite activity when you were a child?
Example: Paul	stuffed animals, cars, balls	baseball

Finding Words in Phrases

As you read, try to notice words in phrases. There are many types of phrases. Here are some.

Examples: They **had a fear of** humans.
verb + noun + preposition

We should **think of this game** as a learning experience.
verb + preposition + noun

Write a **list of questions**.
noun + preposition + noun

E. PRACTICE: FINDING WORDS IN PHRASES Read these sentences. Underline the phrases. Notice the prepositions.

1. Researchers reminded the students of their gender.
2. What was the purpose of the study?
3. What is the cause of the problem?
4. This is a test of memory.
5. You need to fill out a questionnaire.
6. This is a stereotype of Xenrovians.
7. It protected them from danger.
8. The results of the study were interesting.
9. We need to think of this game as practice for adulthood. (Find two phrases.)
10. Researchers came to the conclusion that stereotypes have an effect on us. (Find two phrases.)

F. REVIEW: EDITING A PARAGRAPH There are six mistakes in this paragraph. They are mistakes with punctuation, conjunctions, the phrase *used to*, and prepositions in phrases. Find and correct the mistakes.

When Jane Goodall was 26 years old, Louis Leakey sent her to Tanzania. The purpose of her study was to learn about the wild chimps. She wasn't afraid about them but they were afraid of her. She use to take her binoculars, and sit for many hours every day. Finally, after many months, they let her get close. For almost forty years, she studied the chimps of Gombe. Today, from Goodall's research, we know about chimps' ability to use tools, to be effective mothers and to learn new things.

PART 5 ACADEMIC WRITING

WRITING ASSIGNMENT

In Part 5, you will write one paragraph to answer this question:
- What important lesson did you learn from playing as a child?

MODEL

Here is a model of one student's work. First, just read the model. Don't write anything yet. You will follow these same steps beginning on page 138.

STEP A. CHOOSING A TOPIC Check (✓) one toy, game, activity, or pet that taught you something when you were young. Write your choice.

- ☐ toy ______________________
- ☐ a game ______________________
- ☑ an activity making home movies
- ☐ a pet (cat, dog, etc.) ______________________

STEP B. GETTING IDEAS Answer these questions. Write only short notes.

1. When did you learn this skill or lesson? age 12
2. What was this lesson about? friendship
3. How did you play with this toy, what did you do in this activity or game, or what happened with this pet? Be specific.
   made short movies with action and adventure
   makeup, costumes, video camera
   friends—actors
   scripts
4. What were the steps in your lesson? Put the steps in order. Choose either order of time or order of importance (most important last).
   writer, hero, director—me!
   actors didn't like it
   got angry
   never finished
5. What did you learn? sharing

STEP C. WRITING COMPLETE SENTENCES Take your answers from Steps A and B. Write them in complete sentences. Don't worry about spelling and grammar mistakes. (**Note:** There are some mistakes in the model sentences below.)

- Choose one toy, game, activity, or pet that taught you something when you were young.

  My favorite activity was making movies with my friends.

- Write your notes from Step B in complete sentences.

1. I was 12 years old.
2. I learned a lesson about friendship.
3. My friends and I made short movies with action and adventure.
   We used our older sisters' makeup, made costumes from our parents' old clothes, and used my father's video camera.
   My friends and I were the actors.
   I liked to write, so I used to write the scripts.
4. Things did not go smoothly.
   I wrote the script, and I was also the hero and the director of the movie.
   I gave directions.
   The actors didn't want to listen to me.
   They got angry.
   They lost interest.
   They never finished the movie.
5. I learned the importance of sharing.

STEP D. WRITING YOUR PARAGRAPH On a separate piece of paper, copy your sentences from Step C. You can combine two sentences if you want to. Add a few transition words or details if necessary. Use paragraph form. Indent the first line. After each period, continue on the same line. Don't worry about mistakes.

When I was 12 years old I learned a lesson about friendship from my favorite activity, making movies with my friends. Each movie was only about 10 minutes but the plot was full of action and adventure. We used our older sisters' makeup, made costumes from our parents' old clothes, and used my father's video camera. My friends and I were the actors in these films. I liked to write, so I use to write the scripts. It was fun, but that summer things did not go smoothly. I wrote the script, as usual, and I was also the hero of this movie and the director.

Unfortunately, the actors didn't want to listen to me, when I gave directions. They got angry lost interest and never finished the movie. Why? They were irritated because I wanted to do everything my way. From this experience, I learned the importance of sharing. Nobody likes a bossy friend!

STEP E. EDITING Read your paragraph and look for mistakes with:

- *when*
- punctuation and use of *and, but, or,* and *so*
- *used to*

STEP F. REWRITING Write your paragraph again, without the mistakes.

When I was 12 years old, I learned a lesson about friendship from my favorite activity, making movies with my friends. Each movie was only about 10 minutes, but the plot was full of action and adventure. We used our older sisters' makeup, made costumes from our parents' old clothes, and used my father's video camera. My friends and I were the actors in these films. I liked to write, so I used to write the scripts. It was fun, but that summer things did not go smoothly. I wrote the script, as usual, and I was also the hero of this movie and the director. Unfortunately, the actors didn't want to listen to me when I gave directions. They got angry, lost interest, and never finished the movie. Why? They were angry because I wanted to do everything my way. From this experience, I learned the importance of sharing. Nobody likes a bossy friend!

YOUR TURN

Now follow Steps A–F to write your own paragraph about this question:

• What important lesson did you learn from playing as a child?

STEP A. CHOOSING A TOPIC Check (✓) one toy, game, activity, or pet that taught you something when you were young. Write your choice.

☐ toy ______________________________

☐ a game ______________________________

☐ an activity ______________________________

☐ a pet (cat, dog, etc.) ______________________________

STEP B. GETTING IDEAS Answer these questions. Write only short notes.

1. When did you learn this skill or lesson? ______________________________

2. What was this lesson about? ______________________________

3. How did you play with this toy, what did you do in this activity or game, or what happened with this pet? Be specific.

____

____

____

____

4. What were the steps in your lesson? Put the steps in order. Choose either order of *time* or order of *importance* (most important last).

____

____

____

____

5. What did you learn? ______________________________

STEP C. WRITING COMPLETE SENTENCES Use your answers from Steps A and B. On a separate piece of paper, write them in complete sentences.

STEP D. WRITING YOUR PARAGRAPH On a separate piece of paper, copy your sentences from Step C. You can combine two sentences if you want to. Add a few transition words or details if necessary. Use paragraph form. Indent the first line. After each period, continue on the same line. Don't worry about mistakes.

Writing Strategy

Editing Your Paragraph

Editing is an important step. There are almost always mistakes when you write something the first time. There are two types of mistakes:

- mistakes that *you* can fix
- mistakes that your teacher needs to help with

When you give your paragraph to your teacher, it needs to be as good as you can make it. Your teacher shouldn't have to correct your *careless* mistakes! However, it might be difficult to see your own mistakes. Sometimes it helps to look for specific types of mistakes.

STEP E. EDITING Read your paragraph and look for mistakes with:

- *when*
- punctuation and use of *and, but, or,* and *so*
- *used to*

STEP F. REWRITING Write your paragraph again, without the mistakes.

CHAPTER 6

Becoming a Member of a Community

Discuss the questions.

- Look at the picture. What are the women doing? Why are they happy?
- When does a person become an adult?
- What are some important rituals or ceremonies in life?
- Read the chapter title. What do you think the chapter is about?

PART 1 INTRODUCTION Becoming an Adult

BEFORE READING

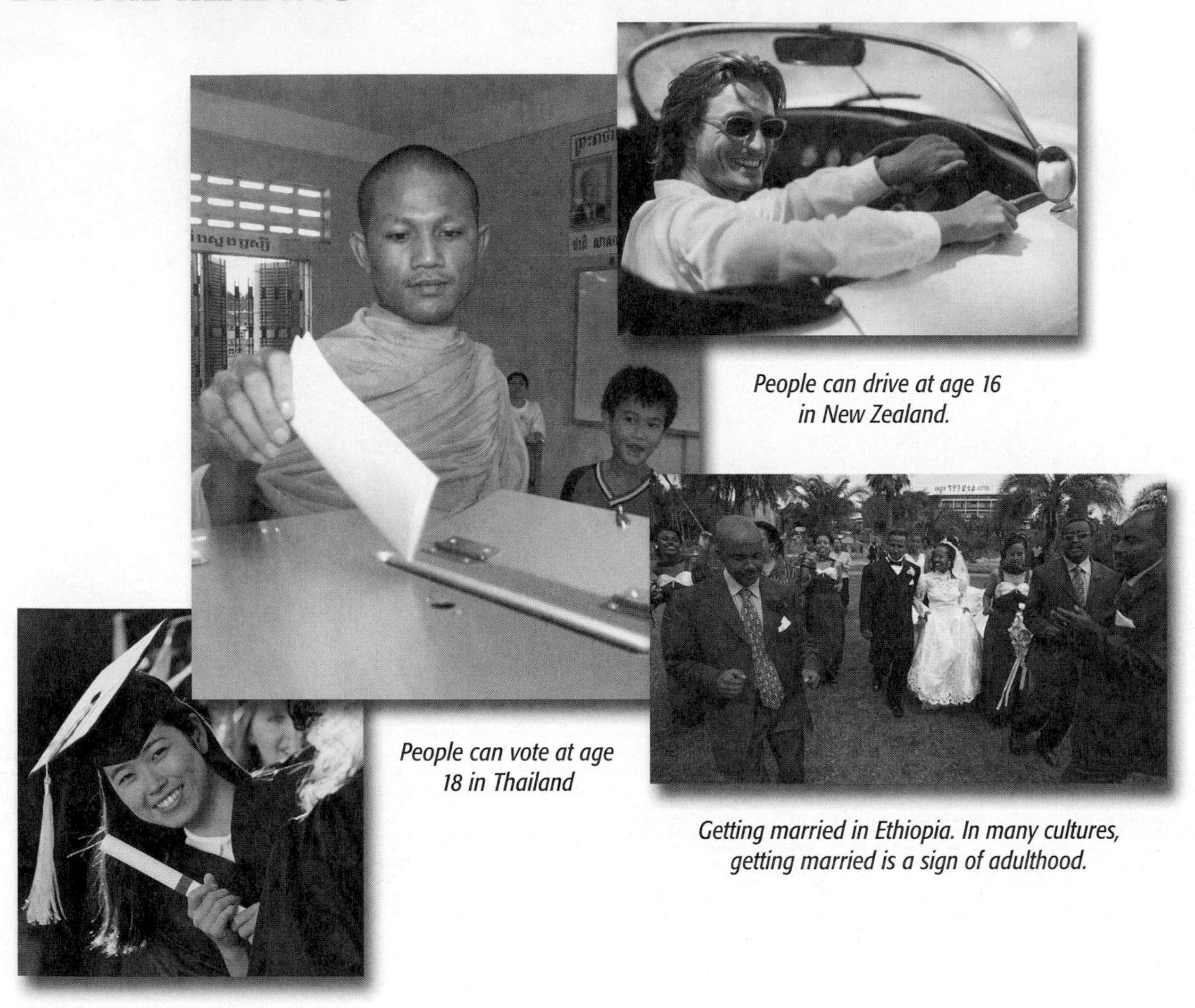

People can drive at age 16 in New Zealand.

People can vote at age 18 in Thailand

Getting married in Ethiopia. In many cultures, getting married is a sign of adulthood.

High school graduation is a big event for many Americans.

THINKING AHEAD Answer these questions with a partner.

1. Do you vote? If yes, when did you first vote? How did you feel the first time you voted?
2. Do you drive? If yes, when did you first drive? How did you feel the first time you drove alone?
3. In your opinion, when is a person an adult?
4. In your opinion, what is an adult? That is, what does "being an adult" mean to you?

READING

Read about becoming an adult. As you read, think about this question:
- What events are signs of adulthood?

Becoming an Adult

In many cultures, specific events are a sign of adulthood. In the United States, for example, young people get to drive around the age 16, graduate from high school around 18, and vote at 18. These events give young people some of the rights (things that they *can* do) and responsibilities (things that they *should* do) of adulthood. Young people in different countries get these rights and responsibilities at different ages. The following chart shows the ages when people can leave school, get married, vote, and drive in several countries around the world.

Country	Minimum (youngest or earliest) Age Permitted to Leave School*	Minimum Marriage Age for Girl/Boy*	Voting Age	Driving Age
Argentina	14	16/18	18	18
Bulgaria	16	16	18	18
Canada	16-18	16*	18	16
Costa Rica	18	18	18	18
Egypt	14	16/18	18	18
Ethiopia	people don't have to go to school	15/18	18	14
Iran	11	15/18	15	18
Italy	16	16	18	18
Japan	15	16/18*	20	18
Korea	15	16/18	17	18
Thailand	around 15	17	18	18
Turkey	14	15/17*	18	18
United States	16	16/17*	18	16

*With parental consent. (Their parents must allow the action.)
Source: "At What Age," Right to Education

AFTER READING

A. CHECK YOUR UNDERSTANDING Which sentences are true? Which sentences are false? Fill in (T) for *True* or (F) for *False*.

1. People in different countries get the rights and responsibilities of adulthood at different ages. (T) (F)
2. Young people can vote at age 15 in Korea. (T) (F)
3. A 16-year-old girl can get married in Thailand. (T) (F)
4. Ethiopians can leave school at any age. (T) (F)
5. Bulgarians can drive at 16. (T) (F)

B. TALK ABOUT IT Answer these questions in small groups.

1. Is any information in the chart surprising to you? Which information? Why?
2. In your opinion, what is the best age to leave school? To get married? To vote? To drive a car?

PART 2 GENERAL INTEREST READING Rites of Passage

BEFORE READING

A. THINKING AHEAD Choose an event: birth, wedding, graduation (finishing school or college), or death. Write it on the line.

My event: ___________________________

What do people do for this event? Think about answers to these questions:

1. What do people wear?
2. What do people eat?
3. Are people alone or in groups?
4. Is there special music?
5. What else do people do?

Now ask four classmates about the event that they chose. Write their answers in the chart on page 145.

Brides and grooms often wear special clothes at their wedding.

Questions	Student 1: ______	Student 2: ______	Student 3: ______	Student 4: ______
What is the event?				
What do people wear?				
What do people eat?				
Are people alone or in groups?				
Is there special music?				

B. VOCABULARY PREPARATION Read the sentences below. The words and phrases in blue are from the next reading. Match the definitions in the box with the words and phrases in blue. Write the correct letters on the lines.

a. the army, navy, or other group that fights for a nation
b. at this time
c. become a member again
d. one or the other
e. place in society
f. people separate from a group
~~g.~~ situation

__g__ **1.** High school graduation is a change from one **condition** in life to another.

_____ **2.** In some cultures, a married person has a higher **social position** than an unmarried person.

_____ **3.** In many rites of passage, the young people leave the group. Later, they **rejoin** it.

_____ **4.** Students are members of a group, but they are also **individuals** with their own ideas.

_____ **5.** You can choose the class at 9 A.M. or the class at 10 A.M.; in other words, you can be in **either** class.

_____ **6.** Anna and Chen put on their formal clothes. Then they went to the church. **At this point**, they were ready for the wedding.

_____ **7.** After high school graduation, Maria is going to join the **military**. She wants to be a soldier.

Reading Strategy

Guessing the Meanings of New Words: *Or*

You don't always need a dictionary to guess the meaning of a new word. Sometimes there is a definition, explanation, or example before or after the word *or*.

Example: At this stage, they are learning the **appropriate** or correct behavior for their new role.

C. GUESSING THE MEANINGS OF NEW WORDS: *OR* As you read, look for the meanings of new words before or after the word *or*.

READING

Read about rites of passage. As you read, think about this question:

- What are some rites of passage?

Rites of Passage

All cultures have rites of passage. A rite of passage is an activity that marks a change in a person's life. In other words, it is a sign of a change or transition from one condition in life to another. It can also be a change in place, social position, or age. Many cultures have **rites of passage** (or rituals) for birth, **initiation** (becoming a member of a group), marriage, and death. For example, graduation is a rite of passage. A wedding is a rite of passage. Many cultures have coming-of-age-rituals, or rites of passage for changing from a child into an adult.

Becoming a Member of a Group

People can join a group—become a member—at different times in life. An example of a birth ritual in many cultures is **naming**—giving a new baby one or more names. Naming rituals often mean two things: the new person is an individual, and he or she is also a member of a group. For example, a first name—Maria—means that the baby is an individual. A last name—Aquino—means that the baby is a member of a specific family group. An example of an initiation ritual is joining a special group such as a club or organization. In some initiation rituals for clubs, students must do certain tasks. After they do the tasks, they are members of the group.

Most rites of passage have three stages, or parts, in the ritual: **separation**, **transition**, and **incorporation**. In the separation stage, people leave a social group and begin to move from one place or position to another place or position. In this stage, they are beginning the rite of passage. They often separate from the rest of society and stop their previous activities. The transition stage is in the middle of the rite of passage. At this stage, people are between groups. They don't belong to either group. At this stage, they are learning the appropriate or correct behavior for their new role—the part they play in the group. In the incorporation stage, people find their new role, and they rejoin the group. At this point, the ritual is finished.

Characteristics of Rites of Passage

Rites of passage have certain characteristics. For example, people in rites of passage often wear special clothing. The clothing symbolizes or marks the change in their role. An example is a bride's white wedding dress. In some cultures, babies also wear a long white dress for a naming ritual. Another example is a graduation cap and tassel.

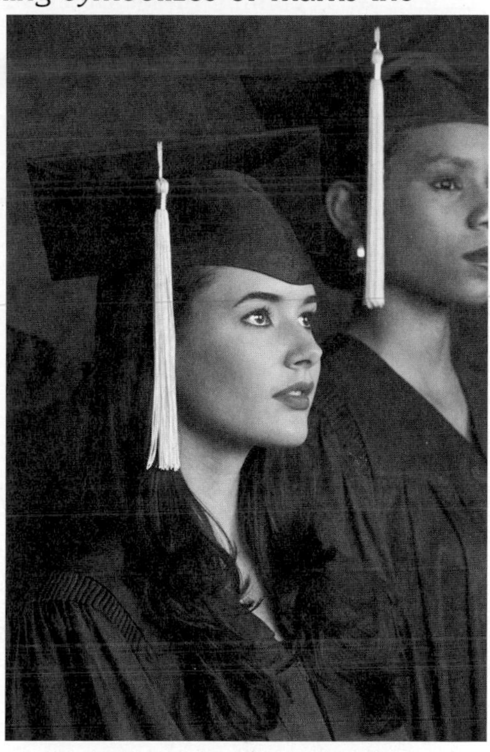

A graduation cap with a tassel on the side

People often have rite-of-passage rituals in groups. Examples of these groups include people who are joining the military and people who are graduating from college. In a North American graduation ceremony, the students sit together in a special area. They are separated from their families and friends. They walk across a stage. This walk symbolizes their transition. Then they move the tassels on their caps from one side to the other. This is symbolic, too. It means that they now belong to the group of college graduates.

In some coming-of-age rituals, young people must have a difficult or challenging experience. They might live alone, outdoors (outside), or without food for a period of time. A young person might also do a difficult task in a coming-of-age ritual. For example, in a coming-of-age ritual among the Apache (a Native American group), a girl must dance early in the morning for many hours without stopping. She also must not eat for four days. In some religions, young people have to memorize a long piece of writing for a coming-of-age ritual. Then they say it for their families and friends. When the young person finishes the challenging task, he or she is ready to be an adult.

Transitions in life can be difficult. Rituals help people with these changes. Rituals can make "life changes" go more smoothly for many people.

AFTER READING

A. CHECK YOUR UNDERSTANDING Which statements are true, according to the reading? Check (✓) the true statements.

______ **1.** A rite of passage is an activity that marks a change in life.

______ **2.** An example of an initiation ritual is a marriage ceremony.

______ **3.** A coming-of-age ritual is a rite of passage for changing from a child to an adult.

______ **4.** A rite of passage has four stages.

______ **5.** Rites of passage can help make some of the changes in life go more smoothly.

B. FINDING DETAILS What are the characteristics of rites of passage? Finish the tree diagram with information from the reading.

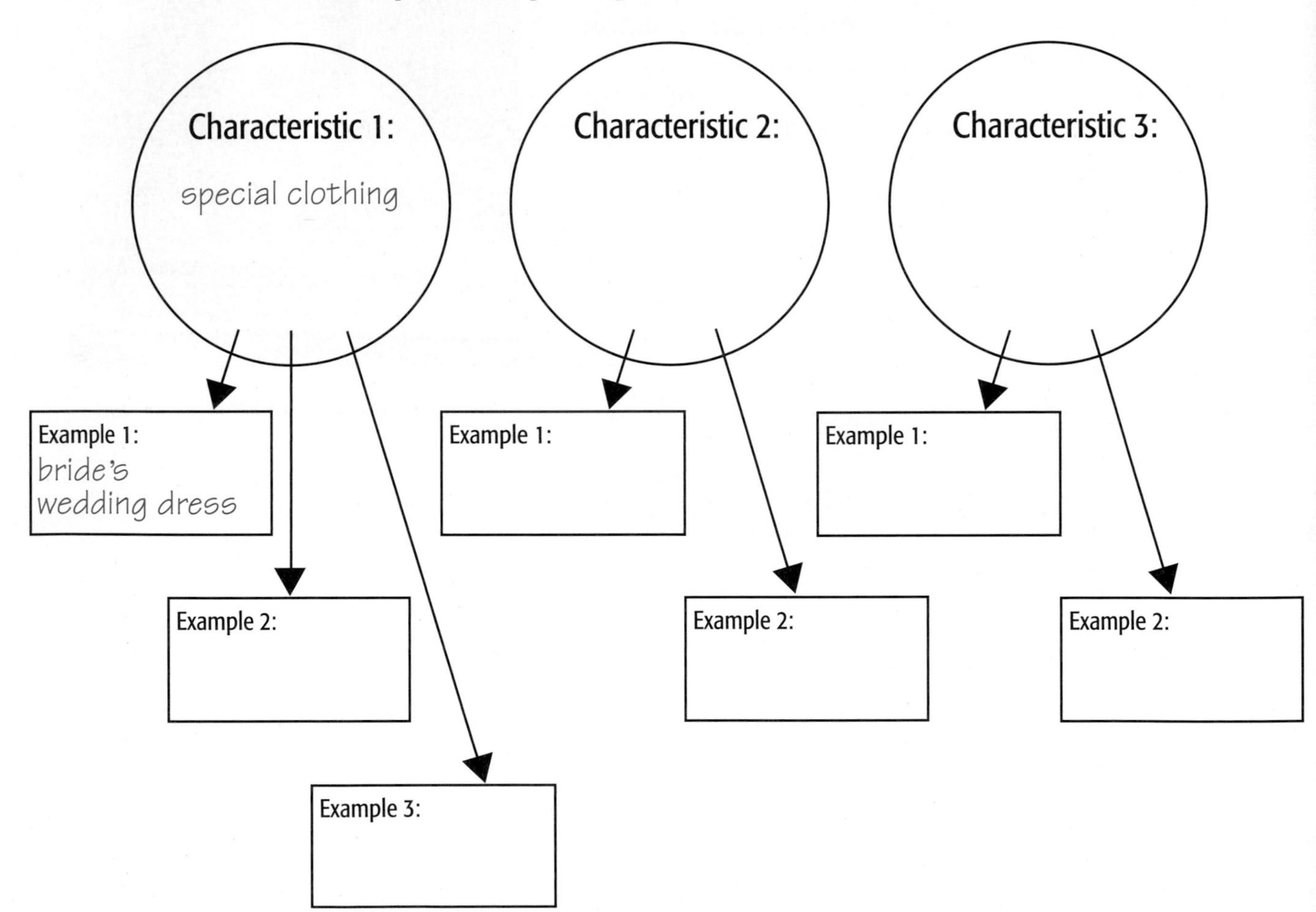

C. VOCABULARY CHECK Fill in the blanks with words from the box.

appropriate	rituals	symbolizes
club	stages	~~transition~~

1. Many cultures have a rite of passage that marks the ___transition___ from childhood to adulthood.
2. Weddings, namings, and graduation ceremonies are all ________________ that mark important events in life.
3. Chris was lonely, so when he went to college, he joined a ________________. The members of the group became his friends.
4. In some cultures, the color black ________________ death. People wear black when someone in their family dies.
5. Young people learn ________________ behavior from their parents and other adults. When they do something wrong, the adult will correct them.
6. Most rites of passage have three ________________. After the third part, the ritual is finished.

Reading Strategy

Recognizing Key Words

Textbooks teach important words and expressions. These are called key words. In textbooks, they are often in **bold** print. A definition or explanation follows them.

Examples: All cultures have **rites of passage**. **A rite of passage is an activity that marks a change in a person's life.**

D. PRACTICE: RECOGNIZING KEY WORDS Look back at the reading on pages 146–147 for key words and their definitions. Then answer the questions.

1. What are the three stages of most rites of passage?
2. What is the first stage in a rite of passage?
3. In which stage do people learn the appropriate behavior for their new role?
4. What do people do in the incorporation stage of a rite of passage?

E. TALK ABOUT IT Work with a partner to describe a rite of passage that you, a friend, or someone in your family experienced. What were the stages? Did it have special clothes? Did people do it in a group? Was it difficult or challenging?

PART 3 ACADEMIC READING Coming-of-Age Rituals

BEFORE READING

Reading Strategy

Using Topic Sentences to Preview

One way to preview a reading is to read the first sentence of each paragraph. These are usually topic sentences. Topic sentences give the main idea of a paragraph.

A. USING TOPIC SENTENCES TO PREVIEW Read the topic sentences in the reading on pages 151–153. Then answer these questions with a partner:

1. Which countries or ethnic groups is the reading about?
2. What kind of information will you learn about each country or culture?
3. What might this reading be about?

B. VOCABULARY PREPARATION Read the sentences below. The words in blue are from the next reading. Match the definitions in the box with the words in blue. Write the correct letters on the lines.

a. beautiful and rich looking	**e. was involved in**
b. learn about	**f. way of living**
~~c.~~ the number of people living in a place	**g. with a lot of rules**
d. a smaller number of	

__c__ **1.** New York City has a large **population**. About 8 million people live there.

____ **2.** In the past, many societies had coming-of-age rituals. Today, **fewer** societies have rites of passage.

____ **3.** Emma wore an **elegant** dress to the party.

____ **4.** College is challenging, but Kofi likes his new **lifestyle**.

____ **5.** Carlos wants to go to clubs at night, but his parents are **strict**. They won't allow it.

____ **6.** Joy is going to live in a new country next year. She wants to **explore** a new culture.

____ **7.** Allison's friend got married last year, and Allison **participated in** the wedding.

Reading Strategy

Guessing the Meanings of New Words: Pictures and Captions

You don't always need a dictionary to guess new words. Sometimes pictures and captions (the words under a picture) help you to understand new words.

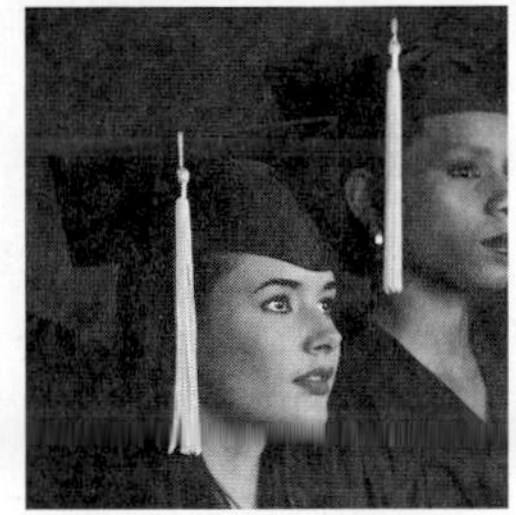

A graduation **cap** *with a* **tassel** *on the side*

C. GUESSING THE MEANINGS OF NEW WORDS: PICTURES AND CAPTIONS As you read, look for meanings of words in pictures and captions.

READING

Read about coming-of-age traditions. As you read, think about this question:

- How do some young people mark their adulthood?

Coming-of-Age Rituals

Many cultures have special rituals to mark adulthood. Some of these are Coming-of-Age Day in Japan; *fiesta de quinceaños* in Latin America and the United States; and *rumspringa* among the Amish, a small religious group in the United States.

Coming-of-Age Day in Japan

In Japan, 20-year-olds have the legal rights of adults. For example, they can vote and get married without parental consent. To celebrate this, many young people participate in Coming-of-Age Day *(Seijin no Hi)*. Coming-of-Age Day is the second Monday in January. It is a national holiday—a holiday for everyone in the country. Even in ancient Japan, there were coming-of-age ceremonies. The modern ceremony, however, began in 1876. In that year, 20 became the legal age of adulthood.

Twenty-year-olds dressed in elegant Kimonos with white fur collars on Coming-of-Age Day

For Coming-of-Age Day, young adults wear formal clothing. Some women wear beautiful kimonos. New kimonos are expensive, so many women do not buy them. They rent them, instead. Kimonos are very difficult to put on, and many women need help getting dressed. Some women also wear white fur collars with their kimonos Young men usually wear business suits. Friends and family take pictures of the young people in their elegant clothes.

A visit to a shrine on Coming-of-Age Day

On this day, 20-year-olds have many activities. First, they go to big outdoor events in their hometowns (their places of birth). If they live in a new town, they return to their hometown for Coming-of-Age Day. At these events, government representatives give speeches and small gifts to the new adults. The speeches explain the rights and responsibilities of adulthood. After the meetings, the 20-year-olds go to parties or to dinner with their friends and family. Many also visit a shrine with family and friends on this day.

Although it's an old ritual, Coming-of-Age Day is changing. The population in Japan gets smaller and smaller every year. Every year, fewer people celebrate it. In addition, the government ceremonies are becoming less popular with young people.

Fiesta de Quinceaños

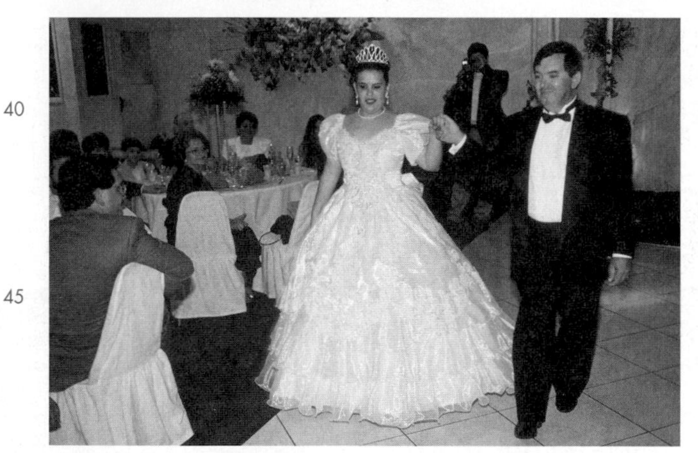
A quinceañera *in an elegant dress and tiara. Her escort wears a tuxedo.*

Many Latino cultures have a special celebration for a girl's fifteenth birthday *(quinceaños)*. She becomes a woman on this day. This event is called *fiesta de quinceaños. Quinceaños* means "fifteen years." The *quinceaños* celebration is a very formal event. The night before a girl's fifteenth birthday, musicians play for her. The *quinceaños* celebration is the weekend after a girl's fifteenth birthday. This celebration is similar to a big church wedding. Everyone wears formal clothing; for example, the boys and men wear tuxedoes, and the girls and women wear elegant party dresses. The *quinceañera* herself wears a long white or pink dress. The girl chooses a boy to be her escort and chooses members of her "court." The court is a group of special friends of the same age, both boys and girls. The court must learn special dances for the event.

There are many events on the day of the *quinceaños* celebration. On the morning of the event, the girl, her family, and her court go to church. After the church ceremony, the big party begins. The celebration includes a dinner. After the dinner, there is dancing. The girl dances first with her father and then with each of the male guests. Often, there are flowers, a large birthday cake, and a photographer to take pictures.

The girl receives symbolic gifts. One is a tiara, a small crown. The tiara means that the girl is special, like a princess. At the end of the evening, a 65 family member puts the tiara on the girl's head. This symbolizes her adulthood.

Amish *Rumspringa*

An Amish family

The Amish are a small religious group in the United States. They came to the United States from Switzerland and Germany in the 1700s. Today, they live mainly in Indiana, Ohio, and 70 Pennsylvania. They live apart from the rest of American society.

The Amish are different from most Americans. They have strict rules. For example, there are rules about clothing and appropriate behavior. 75 Amish wear dark clothes. Most women wear long dresses. Most Amish do not own cars. Instead, they ride in horse-drawn buggies. Most do not allow electricity in their homes, so they don't have TV, computers, or electric lights. Most also 80 do not allow people to take their photograph. They speak their own language, Pennsylvania Dutch, at home. They learn English at school.

An Amish horse-drawn buggy

Most Amish young people have strict lives, but at age 16, things can be different. Most Amish 85 children go to school until the eighth grade (around age 13). They then go to work on their family's farm or in their family's business until they marry. However, when Amish children are 16 years old, their society allows them to 90 explore the non-Amish world, to experience life outside their community. This helps them to decide if they want to stay in the Amish community and to join the Amish church. This rite of passage is called *rumspringa. Rumspringa* means "running around" in Pennsylvania Dutch.

95 During *rumspringa*, Amish teenagers can do whatever they want to do. They drive cars, date, and watch TV. Many have big parties and stay up all night. They can also wear clothing that is not allowed by the Amish, such as jeans and short skirts. Their parents do not tell them what to do during this period. Many even move out of their parents' houses. After this period, most 100 Amish teens—85 to 90 percent—return to their families, their values, and to the Amish lifestyle.

AFTER READING

A. CHECK YOUR UNDERSTANDING Which statements are true, according to the reading? Check (✓) the true statements.

______ **1.** Coming-of-Age Day in Japan celebrates the age when people have the rights of adults.

______ **2.** Coming-of-Age Day is becoming more popular.

______ **3.** The *quinceaños* celebration is a small, quiet, informal event.

______ **4.** In the *quinceaños* celebration, the tiara symbolizes the girl's childhood.

______ **5.** After *rumspringa*, most Amish young people leave the Amish community.

Reading Strategy

Finding Details

Details are specific information about a topic. They are usually facts, examples, or explanations. They usually follow main idea statements.

Examples: During *rumspringa*, Amish boys and girls can do whatever they want to do **(Main Idea Statement)**. They drive cars, date, and watch TV. Many have big parties and stay up all night **(Details)**.

B. PRACTICE: FINDING DETAILS Find details for these ideas in "Coming-of-Age Rituals."

Ideas	Details
In Japan, 20-year-olds have the rights of adults.	They can vote and get married without parental consent.
For Coming-of-Age Day, young adults wear formal clothing.	
Fiesta de quinceaños is a very formal event.	
For the *quinceaños* celebration, the girl receives symbolic gifts.	
The Amish have strict rules.	
Most Amish teenagers return to the Amish way of life.	

C. VOCABULARY CHECK Look at pictures and captions in "Coming-of-Age Rituals." Fill in the blanks with words and phrases from the box.

dating	farms	tiara
escort	horse-drawn buggies	~~tuxedo~~

1. A formal suit for a man is called a ___tuxedo___.
2. Peter and Anna are boyfriend and girlfriend. They are ________________.
3. Anna's ________________, Peter, danced with her during the *quinceaños* celebration.
4. At the end of the *quinceaños* celebration, Anna's father put the ________________ on her head.
5. Many Amish people do not drive cars. Instead, they use ________________.
6. Many Amish families live on ________________.

Reading Strategy

Understanding Words in Phrases: Verbs + Prepositions

Some words in phrases are verb + preposition combinations. To remember the preposition, try to memorize the whole phrase.

Example: Many young people **participate in** Coming-of-Age Day.

D. PRACTICE: WORDS IN PHRASES Find these verb + preposition phrases in the reading on pages 151–153. Underline them. Then match them with the meanings. Write the correct letters on the lines.

a. live apart from	b. move out	~~c.~~ put on	d. stay up

___c___ 1. wear (clothes)

______ 2. leave home

______ 3. not go to bed

______ 4. not live with

Critical Thinking Strategy

Making Comparisons

When you make comparisons, you find similarities and differences between two or more things. Making comparisons can help you organize information in a reading.

E. PRACTICE: MAKING COMPARISONS Compare the rites of passage in "Coming-of-Age Rituals" in small groups. Find similarities and differences to complete the chart.

	Coming-of-Age Day	Fiesta de *Quinceaños*	*Rumspringa*
Purpose or Reason	adulthood		
For boys, girls, or both		girls	
Age for ritual			16
Special clothes	yes (kimonos and business suits)		
Symbolic gifts			no
Party			
Photographs			

F. MAKING CONNECTIONS Work with a partner. Find the characteristics of rites of passage (pages 146–147) in one of the rituals: Coming-of-Age Day, *fiesta de quinceaños*, or *rumspringa*. Answer these questions:

- Are there stages in the rite of passage? If yes, what are they?
- Are there special clothes?
- Do people participate in a group?
- Is there a challenging task?

G. JOURNAL WRITING Choose one of these topics

- Describe a rite of passage that you participated in.
- Describe a rite of passage where you were a guest.
- Describe any rite of passage that you know about.

Write about this topic for five minutes. Don't worry about grammar. Don't use a dictionary.

PART 4 THE MECHANICS OF WRITING

In Part 5, you are going to describe a rite of passage. You will need to use the present tense and chronological order. You might need to use *must* or *have to*, prepositions of place, and phrases with verbs and prepositions. Part 4 will help you learn how to use these.

Review: The Simple Present Tense

Use the simple present tense to describe an event, such as a ritual.

Examples: The priest **blesses** the girl during the *fiesta de quinceaños*.
The students **wear** a cap and gown for the graduation ceremony.

Review: Subject-Verb Agreement

The subject of the sentence must agree with the verb in person (first, second, third) and in number (singular or plural).

Examples: Her **father puts** the tiara on her head.
The **students walk** across the stage.
Yoko and Hiro do not participate in Coming-of-Age Day.

Remember: Two subjects (*Yoko* and *Hiro*) are plural. They use the plural form of the verb (no *s*).

A. PRACTICE: THE SIMPLE PRESENT TENSE Fill in each blank with the correct forms of the verbs in parentheses.

1. In a *quinceaños* celebration, the tiara ____means____ (mean) that the girl is like a princess.
2. In Japan, a 20-year-old __________ (have) the legal rights of an adult.
3. People __________ (attend) big outdoor events for Coming-of-Age Day.
4. Every year, fewer people __________ (celebrate) Coming-of-Age Day.
5. Guests usually __________ (wear) formal clothes at a *quinceaños* celebration.
6. The *quinceañera* and her escort __________ (dance) together at the celebration.
7. During this initiation ceremony, the lights __________ (be) out.

   It __________ (be) dark.

Requirements: *Must* and *Have To*

Use *must* or *have to* + the simple form of the verb for something that is necessary or required.

Examples: The court **must learn** special dances for the *quinceaños* celebration.

In some religions, young people **have to memorize** something for a coming-of-age ritual.

B. PRACTICE REQUIREMENTS: *MUST* AND *HAVE TO* Choose a rite of passage that you know. On a separate piece of paper, write six sentences about what is required in this rite of passage. Use *must* or *have to* in your sentences.

Review: Showing Order

Use order words to show the order of stages or events in a rite of passage.

Examples: **First**, the girl dances with her father.
Then she dances with the other guests.

Order words include:

First,	At first,	At the beginning,	Then
Next,	After that,	After a while,	Finally,
At the end,			

Remember: Don't use a comma after *then*.

C. REVIEW: SHOWING ORDER On a separate piece of paper, use these sentences to write a paragraph. Use the events in the list. Use order words. Begin each sentence with a capital letter. Use a comma if necessary.

First sentence: A high school graduation ceremony has several stages.

Event 1: The students put on caps with tassels and sit in a special area.

Event 2: They listen to speeches about their futures.

Event 3: The principal calls their names, and they walk across the stage.

Event 4: They take their diploma—certificate of completion—and shake hands with the principal.

Event 5: They move the tassels on their caps from one side to the other.

Prepositions of Place

Use prepositions of place to show where things and people are. Prepositions of place help people picture details in their minds. Here are some prepositions of place to describe a rite of passage:

on + body part	She wears a cap **on her head**.
on + place	The teacher stands **on the stage**.
in + body part	She holds a piece of paper **in her hand**.
in + place	They sit together **in the room**.
around + body part	She wears a fur collar **around her neck**.
around + place	They dance **around the room**.
across + place	The students walk **across the stage**.

D. PRACTICE: PREPOSITIONS OF PLACE Look at the picture with a partner. Describe five things that you see. Use prepositions of place.

Words in Phrases: Verb + Preposition Combinations

Some words in phrases are verb + preposition combinations. Try to memorize some verb + preposition combinations and use them when you write.

Example: The students **put on** caps and gowns.

E. PRACTICE: WORDS IN PHRASES Read these sentences. Underline the verb + preposition combinations. Notice the prepositions.

1. For Coming-of-Age Day, many Japanese women <u>put on</u> kimonos.
2. At the end of the *fiesta de quinceaños,* the girl takes off the tiara.
3. During the ritual, the oldest man turns off the lights, so everyone sits in the dark.
4. At the beginning of the celebration, the oldest woman must turn on the music.
5. The students stand up when the teacher asks them a question.
6. After the ceremony, the graduating students sit down again.
7. During *rumspringa*, some Amish teenagers move out of their parents' house.

F. REVIEW: EDITING A PARAGRAPH There are eight mistakes in this paragraph. There are mistakes with punctuation, subject-verb agreement, *must* + the simple form of the verb, and preposition + verb combinations. Find and correct them.

A traditional coming-of-age ceremony for an Apache girl is the Sunrise Dance. For this ritual, an Apache girl ~~have~~ has many challenging tasks. First she must awake very early in the morning. She puts a special dress. Then, she must dances and sings for several hours. Then she must run in four directions. After that, a medicine man bless her. At the end the girl throw a blanket in four directions. At this point, the ceremony is over.

PART 5 ACADEMIC WRITING

WRITING ASSIGNMENT

In Part 5, you will write one paragraph about a rite of passage or ritual that you know.

MODEL

Here is a model of one student's work. First, just read the model. Don't write anything yet. You will follow these same steps beginning on page 164.

STEP A. CHOOSING A TOPIC Check (✓) a rite of passage or ritual that you know. Write your choice.

- ☐ a naming ritual ______
- ☑ an initiation ritual becoming a member of the City College Sports Club
- ☐ a coming-of-age ceremony ______
- ☐ a graduation ceremony ______
- ☐ a wedding ceremony ______

STEP B. GETTING IDEAS Answer these questions. Write only short notes.

1. What type of ritual is it? (This will become your topic sentence.) initiation
2. What is the purpose of the ritual? to become a member of the City College Sports Club
3. What happens during the ritual? What are the stages? What happens first? What happens next? When is the ritual finished?

   sit in gym; wait in dark

   lights on; loud music

   member calls names

   students walk across stage

   member puts key on chain around neck

   they shake hands

   student is now member—sits with other members
4. What are the characteristics of the ritual?
   - Does it happen in a special place? the gym
   - Are there special clothes? blue robe and yellow cap

- Do people do it as a group? yes, students sit together
- Are there symbolic objects? What do they mean? key=excellence
- Is the ritual difficult, or is there a difficult or challenging task? waiting in the dark

STEP C. WRITING COMPLETE SENTENCES Take your answers from Step B. Write them in complete sentences. Don't worry about spelling and grammar mistakes. (**Note:** There are some mistakes in the model sentences below.)

1. To become a member of the Bay City College Sports Club, students must participates in an initiation ritual.
2. Students must put on a blue robe and a yellow cap.
3. They must sit together in a group in their robes and caps.
4. They sit in the gym at night.
5. The lights are off.
6. Someone turns on the lights and plays "We Are the Champions."
7. A group of members sit on a stage in the gym.
8. One member calls each student's name.
9. When the students hear their name, they walk up to and across the stage.
10. The most important member of the club put a key on a chain around each student's neck.
11. The key symbolize excellence.
12. It means that the student plays one sport very well.
13. They shake hands.
14. The student becomes a member of the club.
15. The student sits on the stage with the other members.

STEP D. WRITING YOUR PARAGRAPH On a separate piece of paper, copy your sentences from Step C. You can combine two sentences if you want to. Add a few transition words or details if necessary. Use paragraph form. Indent the first line. After each period, continue on the same line. Don't worry about mistakes.

To become a member of the Bay City College Sports Club, students must participates in an initiation ritual. For the ritual, students must put on a blue robe and a yellow cap. Then they must sit together in a group in their robes and caps in the gym at night. The lights are off, so they have to wait in the dark for several minutes. After that someone turns on the lights and plays "We Are the Champions" very loudly. A group of members sit on a stage in the gym. One member calls each student's name. When the students hear their name, they walk up to and across the stage. Then, the most important member of the club put a key on a chain on each student's neck. The key symbolize excellence. That is, it means that the student plays one sport very well. After that, they shake hands. At this point, the student becomes a member of the club and sits on the stage with the other members.

STEP E. EDITING Read your paragraph and look for mistakes with:

- subject-verb agreement
- punctuation with order words
- *must* and *have to* + the simple form of the verb
- prepositions of place

STEP F. REWRITING Write your paragraph again, without the mistakes.

To become a member of the Bay City College Sports Club, students must participate in an initiation ritual. For the ritual, students must put on a blue robe and a yellow cap. Then they must sit together in a group in their robes and caps in the gym at night. The lights are off, so they have to wait in the dark for several minutes. After that, someone turns on the lights and plays "We Are the Champions" very loudly. A group of members sits on a stage in the gym. One member calls each student's name. When the students hear their name, they walk up to and across the stage. Then the most important member of the club puts a key on a chain around each student's neck. The key symbolizes excellence. That is, it means that the student plays one sport very well. After that, they shake hands. At this point, the student becomes a member of the club and sits on the stage with the other members.

YOUR TURN

Now follow Steps A–F to write your own paragraph about a rite of passage or ritual that you know.

STEP A. CHOOSING A TOPIC Check (✓) a rite of passage or ritual that you know. Write your choice.

- ☐ a naming ritual ______________________________
- ☐ an initiation ritual ______________________________
- ☐ a coming-of-age ceremony ______________________________
- ☐ a graduation ceremony ______________________________
- ☐ a wedding ceremony ______________________________

STEP B. GETTING IDEAS Answer these questions. Write only short notes.

1. What type of ritual is it?

____

2. What is the purpose of the ritual?

____

3. What happens during the ritual? What are the stages? What happens first? What happens next? When is the ritual finished?

____

____

____

____

____

____

____

4. What are the characteristics of the ritual?

- Does it happen in a special place? ______________________________
- Are there special clothes? ______________________________
- Do people do it as a group? ______________________________
- Are there symbolic objects? What do they mean? ______________________________
- Is the ritual difficult, or is there a difficult or challenging task? ______________________________

STEP C. WRITING COMPLETE SENTENCES Take your answers from Step B. On a separate piece of paper, write them in complete sentences. Don't worry about spelling and grammar mistakes.

STEP D. WRITING YOUR PARAGRAPH On a separate piece of paper, copy your sentences from Step C. You can combine two sentences if you want to. Add a few transition words or details if necessary. Use paragraph form. Indent the first line. After each period, continue on the same line. Don't worry about mistakes.

STEP E. EDITING Read your paragraph and look for mistakes with:

- subject-verb agreement
- punctuation with order words
- *must* and *have to* + the simple form of the verb
- prepositions of place

Writing Strategy

Rewriting Your Paragraph

After you edit your paragraph, rewrite it. Write it without the mistakes. This is also a chance to edit again. Ask yourself: Is my paragraph free of mistakes? Did I capitalize and punctuate correctly? Is my paragraph neat? When you can answer "yes," give your paragraph to your teacher.

STEP F. REWRITING Write your paragraph again, without the mistakes.

UNIT 3 VOCABULARY WORKSHOP

Review vocabulary items you learned in Chapters 5 and 6.

A. MATCHING Match the definitions with the words. Write the correct letters on the lines.

Words	Definitions
__e__ **1.** appropriate	**a.** get ready
____ **2.** briefly	**b.** jobs
____ **3.** either	**c.** have a picture in mind
____ **4.** eye contact	**d.** time of changing
____ **5.** imagine	**e.** correct
____ **6.** in the wild	**f.** one or the other
____ **7.** minimum	**g.** for a short time
____ **8.** prepare	**h.** looking into people's eyes
____ **9.** tasks	**i.** in nature
____ **10.** transition	**j.** lowest age or number

B. TRUE OR FALSE? Fill in (T) for *True* or (F) for *False*.

1. A twenty-year-old person is **elderly**. (T) (F)
2. **Siblings** are brothers and sisters. (T) (F)
3. A person's **social position** is his or her place in society. (T) (F)
4. If something is too **general**, it has too many details. (T) (F)
5. **Results** are something that people learn from a scientific study. (T) (F)
6. A **vocal** person is very quiet. (T) (F)
7. A woman who is getting married is a **groom**. (T) (F)
8. A **rite of passage** is an activity that marks a change in a person's life. (T) (F)

C. SENTENCE HALVES Match the first half of the sentences with the correct second half. Write the correct letters on the lines.

__f__ **1.** Researchers study... **a.** to get married in some countries.

____ **2.** You have the right to vote... **b.** in my hometown is getting bigger.

____ **3.** You need parental consent... **c.** society and humans in groups.

____ **4.** The population... **d.** his family.

____ **5.** Kofi lives apart from... **e.** at age 20 in Japan.

____ **6.** A sociologist studies... **f.** a subject to get more information about it.

D. WORDS IN PHRASES: PREPOSITIONS Which prepositions can you put together with the words in blue? Fill in the blanks with words from the box. Use two of these prepositions more than once.

in	of	on	out	to	up

1. The teacher asked the students to **fill** ___out___ a questionnaire.
2. The researchers **came** ________ the conclusion about stereotypes.
3. Negative stereotypes can have a negative **effect** ________ people.
4. Many young people **participate** ________ graduation ceremonies.
5. Naomi **put** ________ her jacket and went outside.
6. Ken hopes to **return** ________ his hometown next year.
7. Kirsten has an exam tomorrow, so she's going to **stay** ________ all night and study.
8. At Nina's event, a photographer is going to **take pictures** ________ the guests.

APPENDIX 1 SPELLING RULES

Rules for adding an *-s* for the plural form and the third person singular of verbs in the simple present tense:

1. Add *-es* to words that end in *-ch, -s, -sh, -x,* or *-z.*

catch	→	catches
kiss	→	kisses
push	→	pushes
fix	→	fixes
buzz	→	buzzes

2. If the simple form of a verb ends in a consonant + *y,* change the *y* to *i* and add *-es.*

fly	→	flies
study	→	studies

   Note: Do not change the *y* or add an *e* if the simple form ends in vowel + *y.*

enjoy	→	enjoys
stay	→	stays

3. For most other verbs, just add *-s.*

think	→	thinks
put	→	puts

Rules for adding *-ing:*

1. If the simple form of the verb ends in a silent *-e,* drop the *-e* and add *-ing.*

move	→	moving
write	→	writing

2. If the simple form ends in *-ie,* drop the *-ie,* add *y* and the *-ing.*

die	→	dying
lie	→	lying

3. If the last three letters are consonant/vowel/consonant in a one-syllable word, double the last consonant and then add *-ing.*

put	→	putting
run	→	running
drop	→	dropping

   Note: Do not double *w, x,* or *y.*

4. For a two-syllable word that ends in consonant/vowel/consonant, there are two rules:

   a. If the accent is on the second syllable, double the final consonant.

      permit → permitting

   b. If the accent is on the first syllable, do not double the final consonant.

      happen → happening

5. For all other verbs, simply add *-ing.* Do not drop, add, or change anything.

work	→	working
study	→	studying

Rules for adding *-ed* for the past tense or past participle of regular verbs:

1. If the verb already ends in *-e*, just add *-d.*

move	→	moved
tie	→	tied

2. If the verb ends in consonant + *y*, change the *y* to *-ied.*

hurry	→	hurried
study	→	studied

Note: Do not change the *y* to *-ied* if the verb ends in vowel + *y.*

enjoy	→	enjoyed
stay	→	stayed

3. If the last three letters are consonant/vowel/consonant in a one-syllable word, double the last consonant and then add *-ed.*

rub	→	rubbed
stop	→	stopped

Note: Do not double *w, x,* or *y.*

4. For a two-syllable word that ends in consonant/vowel/consonant, there are two rules:

   a. If the accent is on the second syllable, double the final consonant.

permit	→	permitted

   b. If the accent is on the first syllable, do not double the final consonant.

happen	→	happened

5. For all other regular verbs, simply add *-ed.*

learn	→	learned
want	→	wanted

APPENDIX 2 COMMON IRREGULAR VERBS

Simple Present	Simple Past	Past Participle
am/is/are	was/were	been
beat	beat	beat
become	became	become
begin	began	begun
break	broke	broken
bring	brought	brought
buy	bought	bought
catch	caught	caught
choose	chose	chosen
come	come	come
cost	cost	cost
cut	cut	cut
do	done	done
draw	drew	drawn
drink	drank	drunk
drive	drove	driven
eat	ate	eaten
hear	heard	heard
fall	fell	fallen
feed	fed	fed
feel	felt	felt
find	found	found
fly	flew	flown
forget	forgot	forgotten
freeze	froze	frozen
get	got	gotten/got
give	gave	given
go	went	gone
grow	grew	grown
hit	hit	hit
hold	held	held
keep	kept	kept
know	knew	known
lay	laid	laid
leave	left	left
lend	lent	lent
lose	lost	lost
make	made	made

Simple Present	Simple Past	Past Participle
mean	meant	meant
meet	met	met
pay	paid	paid
put	put	put
read	read	read
ride	rode	ridden
ring	rang	rung
rise	rose	risen
run	ran	run
say	said	said
see	saw	seen
send	sent	sent
set	set	set
shake	shook	shaken
show	showed	shown
shut	shut	shut
sing	sang	sung
sink	sank	sunk
sit	sat	sat
sleep	slept	slept
speak	spoke	spoken
spend	spent	spent
stand	stood	stood
steal	stole	stolen
stick	stuck	stuck
sweep	swept	swept
swim	swam	swum
take	took	taken
teach	taught	taught
tear	tore	torn
tell	told	told
think	thought	thought
throw	threw	thrown
wake	woke	woken
wear	wore	worn
win	won	won
wind	wound	wound
write	wrote	written

SKILLS INDEX

VOCABULARY INDEX

Chapter 1
adult
careful
costumes
creative
design
determine
entertainment
friendly
happy
hard worker
hero
identity
inherit
middle-class
normal
outgoing
plot
reader
role
serious
setting
share
shy
upper-class
whatever

Chapter 2
academic material
active
approach
bilingual dictionary
bits
challenging
chunks
commands
essay
focus on
memorize
mnemonic
multiple-choice
neurons
passage
phrases
physical actions
physically
problem-solving exercises
respond
short-answer
solution
stimulation
strategies
target language
true/false

Chapter 3
acquire
admire
advertising
advice
ancient
archeologist
aware of
career
commercials
counselor
crazy about
(the) distant past
don't matter
experts
gender
however
involves
mentally
mentors
moments
moral characteristics
passion
passive
profession
psychology
role models
smoothly
talent
unfortunately
wealth

Chapter 4

appeals to
attract
belong to
clicking a button
effective
fact of life
fans
here to stay
highlights
high-performance
image
improve
income
irritating
junk
market
name brands
outdoor displays
packaging
personalize
qualities
reflect
specific
town criers
trademark
values

Chapter 5

adulthood
amount
choice
daughter
elderly
eye contact
general
grocery store
imagine
infants
prepare
races
relationships
researchers
results
sociologists
son
stereotype
take apart
tasks
vocal
worse

Chapter 6

appropriate
at this point
club
condition
dating
either
elegant
escort
explore
farms
fewer
horse-drawn buggies
individuals
lifestyle
live apart from
military
move out
participated in
population
put on
rejoin
rituals
social position
stages
stay up
strict
symbolizes
tiara
transition
tuxedo

CREDITS

Photo Credits

Cover background corridor: © Stockbyte/PunchStock; student in library: Bananastock/PictureQuest; graduation: © Digital Vision; leopard: Getty Images; **p. 1** BananaStock/PictureQuest; **p. 3** Getty Images; top: Corbis Royalty-Free; middle/bottom: Getty Images; **p. 5** Thomas Wanstall/The Image Works; **p. 7** top: © Josef Scaylea/CORBIS; middle: © Bettmann/CORBIS; bottom: Sasha/Getty Images; **p. 9** Time Life Pictures/Getty Images; **p. 12** © Digital Vision; **p. 14** RubberBall/PictureQuest; **p. 16** Getty Images; **p. 18** © Corbis/PunchStock; **p. 29** BananaStock/PictureQuest; **p. 30** Getty Images; **p. 53** Getty Images; **p. 55** © Digital Vision; **p. 56** top/middle: Getty Images; bottom: Corbis Royalty-Free; **p. 60** Corbis/PictureQuest; **p. 61** Digital Vision/Getty Images; **p. 74** top left: Getty Images; top right/bottom left: Corbis Royalty-Free; bottom right: Getty Images; **p. 81** © David Cumming; Eye Ubiquitous/CORBIS; **p. 82** Getty Images; **p. 83** left: Universal/Jersey Films/The Kobal Collection; right: Universal/Everett Collection; **p. 86** top left: AFP/Getty Images; top right/bottom: David N. Averbach; **p. 89** Milwaukee Public Museum; **p. 91** left/right: Image courtesy of The Advertising Archives; **p. 92** top left/top right/bottom: Image courtesy of The Advertising Archives; **p. 94** The McGraw-Hill Companies, Inc./Christopher Kerrigan, photographer; **p. 95** Columbia/The Kobal Collection; **p. 111** © Digital Vision; **p. 113** Richard Koek/Getty Images; **p. 114** top: © Karl Ammann/CORBIS; bottom: James Balog/Getty Images; **p. 115** top: © Brand X Pictures/PunchStock; bottom: Getty Images; **p. 116** Hugo Van Lawick/The Jane Goodall Institute; **p. 119** left/right: Corbis Royalty-Free; **p. 120** Jeff Albertson/CORBIS; **p. 126** © Digital Vision; **p. 127** Getty Images; **p. 141** © Digital Vision; **p. 142** top left: Reuters/CORBIS; top right: Getty Images; bottom left: Bill Losh/Getty Images; bottom right: Michael S. Lewis/CORBIS; **p. 144** Getty Images; **p. 147** Corbis Royalty-Free; **p. 151** top: Corbis Royalty-Free; bottom: Obremski/CORBIS; **p. 152** top: Reuters/CORBIS; bottom: Patrick Ward/CORBIS; **p. 153** top: Sylvain Grandadam/Getty Images; bottom: Getty Images.

We apologize for any apparent infringement of copyright and if notified, the publisher will be pleased to rectify any errors or omissions at the earliest opportunity.